DEADLY BETRAYAL

DEADLY BETRAYAL

The Truth About Why The United States Invaded Iraq

DENNIS FRITZ

O/R

OR Books
New York · London

© 2024 Dennis Fritz

Published by OR Books, New York and London

Visit our website at www.orbooks.com

All rights information: rights@orbooks.com

First printing 2024

Library of Congress Cataloging-in-Publication Data: A catalog record for this book is available from the Library of Congress.

British Library Cataloging in Publication Data: A catalog record for this book is available from the British Library.

Typeset by Lapiz Digital. Printed by BookMobile, USA, and CPI, UK.

paperback ISBN 978-1-68219-437-9 • ebook ISBN 978-1-68219-438-6

Immediately prior to this book going to press, the author received a communication from the Defense Office of Prepublication and Security Review at the Pentagon insisting on a number of redactions. With the author's approval the publisher has obscured the text to be redacted with black blocks that appear throughout. The same Pentagon office stipulated that the disclaimer below should appear in the book:

"Simply stated, there is no doubt that Saddam Hussein now has weapons of mass destruction."
—Vice President Dick Cheney, August 2002

Contents

This book is dedicated to the men and women of our Armed Forces, who fight the unjust wars perpetrated by our politicians. Thank you for your sacrifice. May God bless us and forgive our government of its sins.

Foreword

In the first decade of the 2000s, Command Chief Master Sergeant Dennis Fritz and I endured many of the same tribulations generated by the wars in Afghanistan and Iraq. Dennis from his perch at the top of the USAF's non-commissioned officer ranks and as a trusted confidant of the then-chairman of the Joint Chiefs of Staff, General Richard Myers; I as chief of staff to then-secretary of state Colin Powell—who himself had been the military chairman from 1989 to 1993, when I had served as his special assistant. Powell and I had worked closely together on military operations in Panama in 1989–90 and in Iraq in 1990–91. We had also worked together at the end of Powell's years as chairman on the humanitarian operations in Somalia, operations that at the very end of Powell's time as chairman—in fact, three days after he left the position and handed it over to General John Shalikashvili—turned very much into a similar disaster as would come later in Afghanistan and Iraq. This disaster, however, was under the presidential hands of another grossly inexperienced U.S. president, William J. Clinton. Bad American military actions seem to owe allegiance to no particular political party.

From roughly 2004–08, Dennis observed the George W. Bush administration—particularly its secretary of defense,

Donald Rumsfeld and his immediate assistant undersecretary for policy Douglas Feith—from his close vantage point inside the Pentagon. I saw the administration and the Pentagon from my perch at the Department of State. When we met several years later, we were somewhat stunned at the coincidence in our views of both the Administration as a whole and its Defense and State Departments. Likewise, our views of the disastrous wars in Afghanistan and Iraq and of the more pervasive "Global War on Terrorism."

We discovered this coincidence of view through sheer serendipity; or fate if you happen to be the least bit religious or disposed to a very ancient Greek view of the human condition. In immediate retirement, Dennis, wanting very much to continue to serve the men and women of his beloved Air Force, had assumed a vital position at the newly christened Walter Reed National Military Medical Center in Bethesda, Maryland, as the USAF's "Wounded Warrior" program representative, in fullest swing after so many years of two brutal wars. In fact, the first of his wards to whom Dennis introduced me in the lobby of the central medical building was the USAF's only triple amputee, an ordnance expert who had been disarming an Improvised Explosive Device (IED) when it exploded and he lost both his legs and most of his right arm.

I had come to the hospital at Dennis' invitation, which he had extended to me after hearing me register publicly in late 2005 some strong criticism of the Iraq War, almost a year following my departure from government. He wanted me to be able to see some of that war's tragic results, to reinforce my distaste for the war and for the people who had created it. Dennis succeeded in that regard. After that first visit I emailed him that "Every insight gained is helpful—insight both into the plight of our veterans and into the hubris, hypocrisy, lying, and deceit that brought them to their wounds . . . " From that point on, we became close friends and shared what we knew about our national leaders' decision-making leading to and undergirding this interminable period of brutal war.

Almost from the very beginning of our conversations, I detected a degree of excitement in Dennis that seemed to grow as we met and talked further about the wars and our experiences. It finally revealed itself for what it was when I mentioned my own thoughts about writing a book about my entire experience, from 1989 when I first joined Powell at the US Army's Forces Command, to the four-plus years at State, ending in early 2005. It seemed Dennis too was considering such a project. In fact, he had already compiled rough notes, photographs, made outlines, and had a general concept for the book in mind. Almost eagerly, he displayed these things to me. I was impressed that he had been able to consolidate his preliminary thoughts and material to support them so swiftly and in such an organized manner.

I discovered too that one of the aspects of such an endeavor that troubled Dennis deeply, also troubled me. We both were profoundly concerned how our written efforts, were they to turn into published books, would affect the two people we most admired, regardless of their human frailties—Richard Myers and Colin Powell. To that point, I confided in Dennis, it had been a show-stopper for me, though I too was gathering material and composing outlines. It was clear to me that he too was agonizing. Both of us were well aware that if we were to be as faithful as possible to our main mission—telling the truth about these wars and how they came about and were so badly managed—we could not omit our own culpability and, more significantly by far, that of our superiors, Myers and Powell.

Somehow, Dennis dealt with his inner self and we have arrived at this work. It is the result of that mental wrestling, that powerful dedication and, most of all, the indomitable spirit of this true warrior and his desire to lay bare the facts. I know that he had several conversations with his old friend and mentor, General Myers; but I have not, for reasons obvious to me at least, delved deeply into what transpired. I knew enough about the commitment and character of this man to understand that at the end of the day he would make the decision he felt was correct. I also knew—powerfully so—that Dennis' ultimate loyalty and dedication is to the enlisted men and women and the Non-Commissioned Officers of the United States Air Force, and by extension to all of America's "soldiers"—and especially those wounded in body and spirit, or killed in these utterly stupid wars. Thus, the very apposite title for this book: *Deadly Betrayal*.

The book is well worth reading. Sooner rather than later, in my view, historians will write the complete and accurate history of these disastrous wars from start to finish, and sordid will it be. Alas, however, as with most history that is as accurate as humans can make it, those guilty of the crimes and ravages it inevitably encompasses, will have escaped all but a divine providence's justice. This book at least will perhaps disturb their present comfort. It does mine.

Lawrence Wilkerson, Col, USA (Ret)
Falls Church, Virginia

Introduction: My Personal Odyssey

"If there is a book that you want to read, but it hasn't been written yet, then you must write it."

—Toni Morrison

I served in the United States Air Force for nearly thirty years, the last ten as a senior leader. I held two of the highest enlisted positions in the Air Force, Senior Advisor to the Commander of Pacific Air Forces and Command Chief Master Sergeant of Air Force Space Command, and represented a cumulative total of more than 100,000 service men and women during the latter part of my career. I led with integrity, and advocated tirelessly for the enlisted personnel, speaking out on the issues that affected their health and well being. I was also a senior advisor to four-star generals at three major military commands, analyzing our national security strategy and foreign policy as I worked alongside some of the most significant military leaders of our time: General Richard Myers, former chairman of the Joint Chiefs of Staff; General John Lorber, former Pacific Air Forces commander; General Michael P. C. Carns, former vice chief of staff of the Air Force and a Clinton nominee for CIA director; and Lieutenant General Buster Glosson, war hero and architect of the Desert Storm air campaign, the first military operations against Saddam Hussein, under President George H. W. Bush.

My odyssey has taken me from the top of Earth in Thule, Greenland, to the bottom of the planet in Australia, and I'm blessed to have met numerous presidents and foreign leaders along the way. I've even had the honor of flying on Air Force One, the most famous plane in the world. I also went on a number of trips with members of Congress, including a fact-finding mission in the Middle East prior to the start of Desert Storm.

One of my most memorable encounters was with the late Lloyd Bentsen, senator from Texas and the Democratic vice-presidential nominee in the 1988 election. Bentsen's claim to fame is the legendary retort during a vice presidential debate he hurled at his rival, Senator Dan Quayle, after Quayle compared himself to President John F. Kennedy. "Senator, I served with Jack Kennedy," said Benton. "I knew Jack Kennedy. Jack Kennedy was a friend of mine. Senator, you're no Jack Kennedy."

Senator Bentsen offered me a compliment I'll never forget. He said he was very impressed with my "grasp of the issues," and gave me some advice about a potential future he saw for me. He said when I thought the time was right, I needed to take advantage of my unique talents and run for political office. I think he saw me as a friend.

My grasp of the issues comes from closely studying correspondence and attentively listening to the policymakers around me for more than forty years as I went back and forth between the Pentagon and Washington, D.C. and operational command headquarters. While working in Congressional Affairs for the Air Force in the Pentagon, I was introduced to the legislative process. When I was employed in the Office of the Secretary of Defense, I deepened my awareness of foreign and national security policy formulation. These experiences prepared me for one of my biggest tasks: joining a specially selected team responsible for locating, retrieving, and declassifying Afghanistan and Iraq war planning documents.

However, my proudest professional accomplishment was the time I spent at the Department of Defense's Wounded Warrior Program.

***

On October 23, 2008, while sitting in my office at the Pentagon, I received an email from an old friend and boss, Jim Hawkins, a retired major general who hired me in 2000 to be his senior advisor on the welfare and readiness of the enlisted personnel assigned to Andrews Air Force Base, home of Air Force One. *Chief, I need your help,* he wrote. Hawkins explained that an associate of his was seeking someone with my type of leadership experience to manage the care of war-wounded Air Force personnel convalescing at Walter Reed Army Medical Center in Washington D.C., and later, after a relocation to Maryland, the Walter Reed National Military Medical Center at Bethesda. This position was created by the President's Commission on the Care for America's Returning Wounded Warriors, also known as the Dole-Shalala Commission. The commission wanted to assign an advocate to each wounded warrior and their families in order to help them navigate the cumbersome bureaucracy.

I told Hawkins that sounded like a job for me.

I was offered and accepted the position and started work on November 13, 2008. I fought feverishly to ensure that our wounded warriors received the attention they truly deserved. In time, I would go on to become a recognized expert in Wounded Warrior case management and the face of the Air Force for wounded warrior and family support care at Walter Reed. In 2014, I became the deputy manager, then program manager for the Army's Wounded Warrior Program, supervising more than 100 Wounded Warrior Advocates who provided support services at military treatment facilities, warrior transition units, and VA hospitals throughout the country. In May 2022, I concluded my service to the nation as the contracted program manager for the Department of Defense's Wounded Warrior Recovery Care Program.

These different positions within Wounded Warriors gave me the chance to witness firsthand what our combat heroes and their families endured while fighting to recover from the devastating physical and emotional toll of the Iraq War—a conflict that wasn't about protecting our national security, but was instead about serving a political agenda. Sadly, the courageous individuals who volunteered to defend our country were disregarded as "boots on the ground" by members of our government, and used as pawns by some of the very same politicians who had the audacity to send them off to risk their lives in an ill-advised war.

Many of the people responsible for this catastrophe—Dick Cheney, Donald Rumsfeld, Douglas Feith, George Tenet, Paul Brenner—have penned memoirs to defend their reputations or blame others for their mistakes. This book is different. What you are about to read is an honest account of why we went to war, authored by a career military man, not a politician or a Bush administration mouthpiece, who followed the Pentagon's paper trail to uncover the truth about why we invaded Iraq. *Deadly Betrayal* will help people understand how a select group of government officials formulated and executed the strategy to invade Iraq. We can't allow any self-serving war hawks to manipulate us ever again. We must hold them accountable.

Many friends and associates have urged me to share my story. However, I didn't take them up on it until I came to the conclusion that it could help our troops understand why they were sent to Iraq. Knowing what I know, I realized that I had to write this book. I talked to my minister, my immediate family, and a few close friends, and got their blessings and encouragement. Then I prayed, and off I went. I wrote this book for all audiences, in particular those who aren't versed in American foreign policy and military strategy, although those who are will also get a lot out of reading this account.

Within these pages, many questions about the motive behind the Iraq War will finally be answered.

CHAPTER 1

Granny Was Right

"My fellow citizens, at this hour, American and coalition forces are in the early stages of military operations to disarm Iraq."
— President Bush's opening statement of his address to the nation, March 19, 2003

On January 20, 2001, George W. Bush was sworn in as the forty-third president of the United States. I'll never forget that cold and rainy day. For one thing, my wife and I had the honor of attending a farewell reception for President Bill Clinton and First Lady Hillary Clinton at Andrews Air Force Base. Unexpectedly, I had to help former Secretary of State Madeleine Albright, the first female secretary of state, off the floor: she had slipped on a wet spot and suffered a nasty fall (she was fine, just a little embarrassed). Most importantly, that day has stayed in my mind because my mother-in-law, Mary M. Johnson, said to me, "Get ready, Bush is planning to start a war." I wondered why she would say such an odd thing, but at the time, I paid no heed to her prediction, never imagining it would come to fruition. Nowadays, I often think about what Granny, as she was affectionately called, had said. How did she know?

Fast-forward to the morning of September 11, 2001, a beautiful, crisp sunny day. I was leaving my weekly meeting with Andrews Air Force Base's first sergeants—the enlisted advisors to the organizational commanders—and heading back to the 89th Air Wing headquarters, which was responsible for the operations, maintenance, and security of Air Force One and other aircraft that supported the president, the vice president, Cabinet members, and Congress. Before I could get into my vehicle, however, one of the sergeants, Pab, ran frantically toward me, yelling for me to stop. He then informed me of the horrific news: the Twin Towers of the World Trade Center had been hit by two airliners, and it didn't look like an accident. He also said there were reports that other planes were unaccounted for and possibly heading to Washington. "What is this, Chief?" Pab asked, panic-stricken. "What is happening?"

I was his leader, but had no answers.

I immediately jumped into my vehicle and rushed back to our base headquarters, straight into the office of my boss, General Glenn Spears, the senior commander of the 89th Air Wing. When I got to Spears's office, I was told that the Pentagon had just been attacked. I quickly thought about my friend and former boss, Gen. Richard Myers, who at the time was the vice chairman of the Joints Chiefs of Staff (the second-highest-ranking senior general officer in the military); my brother-in-law Maurice Johnson; one of my best friends, James Cummings; and the many others I knew at the Pentagon from my two previous assignments there. However, my immediate concern was for the safety of the personnel and their families assigned to Andrews. It was common knowledge that Andrews was home to Air Force One.

My mind was racing, gripped with uncertainty: Could we be next, even though Air Force One was scheduled to be in Florida with President Bush, that day? I was worried about the crew. The welfare of Air Force One's flight attendants, security forces, communicators, and maintenance staff rested squarely on my shoulders. Would they be able to return to Andrews if D.C. was possibly under attack? After all, we were only fourteen miles outside of Washington, and we didn't know what was coming next.

As Spears, his key staff, and I watched the Pentagon ablaze on live television, he turned to me and said, "This is war!" We promptly put the base under lockdown. *Could this be the war Granny had predicted?* But after pondering this for a few minutes, I felt that, no, that couldn't possibly be the case. President Bush wouldn't do such a thing. After all, we were attacked with no provocation on our part. However, whoever the culprit was, we had to defend ourselves.

***

In the chaotic months following 9/11, I, like most Americans, wholeheartedly agreed that we should go after Al-Qaeda in Afghanistan. We were told that the Taliban had offered Osama Bin Laden refuge and wouldn't turn him over to us. In our lifetime, we had never witnessed such a vicious attack on our mainland. We wanted retaliation. Three thousand people perished that grim September day. Naturally, we had to punish whoever was responsible, and if that meant taking on the Taliban to capture Bin Laden, then the Bush administration had our support.

It was only later that I learned that invading Afghanistan wasn't merely swift retribution for 9/11, but was rather part of a long-simmering tactic to fulfill a broader agenda: conquering Iraq and other countries in the Middle East and Africa. On March 19, 2003, the first American bombs hit Iraq. Bush started the war Granny had prophesied. Why was this happening? Iraq hadn't attacked us—we weren't at risk because of Saddam Hussein. Even with the limited knowledge I possessed at the time, I still disagreed with the decision to invade Iraq—the reasons given just didn't make sense. In silent protest, I retired from the Air Force. I had always maintained the importance of honesty with the troops. I couldn't look them in the eye and tell them that attacking Iraq was the right thing to do before sending them off to risk their lives.

My disagreement with the war haunted me for years. Even though weapons of mass destruction were never found, I couldn't fault Bush or his administration. I doubted I would ever understand all the reasons we went to war. Then, something unforeseen happened, an act of fate that would open my eyes.

In July 2005, I was recruited and offered a special project position in the Office of the Under Secretary of Defense for Policy. In the chain of command, it was the third-most powerful office in the Pentagon, behind the Secretary and the Deputy Secretary of Defense. The office was led by Douglas Feith, one of the architects who built the case for the Iraq War.

***

I was hired as a research fellow and analyst for the newly created Declassification Review Team (DRT). The DRT was established to identify and review all classified Iraq War policy-planning documents and vet them for declassification and future release through Freedom of Information Act requests or Congressional inquiries. At first, we were directed to home in on documents dealing specifically with the policy and planning relating to Operation Iraqi Freedom, which was the invasion of Iraq.[1] We were later instructed to

---

1   Memo: Declassification Review of Second Iraq War Analyses and Planning Documents, December 22, 2004.

expand our research and analysis to documents concerning Al-Qaeda and Operation Enduring Freedom, the war against the Taliban in Afghanistan.[2]

I was passionate about my work. For me, it wasn't just a job—I was on a mission to get the facts. Because of my dedication, my team regarded me as the person who knew how to identify the most crucial documents. I was awestruck at the treasure trove of data to which we were given access, including personal notes containing shocking revelations as to why we truly went to war in Iraq. I consider these documents as damning as the Pentagon Papers.

Some background: the Pentagon Papers were a top-secret Department of Defense study examining the US government's decision-making regarding the Vietnam War. The papers were leaked by Daniel Ellsberg, a former military analyst, to *The New York Times* and published in 1971. They revealed that the Johnson administration had misled the American public and Congress about its intentions in Vietnam. As the DRT began declassifying the Iraq War documents, I saw that history was being repeated. The government was lying to the American people.

One of my co-workers said, "These individuals can't be that smart, because the fucking idiots put it all on paper and left a trail." I learned that Secretary of Defense Donald Rumsfeld liked putting his thoughts on paper so that he and his deputies could later analyze and even rewrite them, if

---

2   Memo: Declassification Review of Specified Policy Analyses and Planning Documents, May 25, 2005.

necessary. Rumsfeld also did this for his personal historical records. Many of Rumsfeld's memos, which I reviewed, were known as "snowflakes." These were a flurry of tasks typed on plain white bond paper that flew out of his office like a blizzard, straight into the hands of Pentagon staff or combatant commanders. What came to light while analyzing these documents was that our government had framed the Iraq War as an act of self-defense, or, more specifically, as an act of "anticipatory self-defense" against the threat of WMD. It was also touted as an effort to liberate the Iraqi people from Saddam Hussein's tyranny, as Doug Feith stated in his book *War and Decision*. However, as the record will show, all of these claims were pure fabrications.

CHAPTER 2

9/11 and Afghanistan:
The Throughway to Iraq

"I truly am not that concerned about him [Bin Laden]."
— President George W. Bush, speaking at a
press conference on March 13, 2002

After the attack on the Twin Towers and the Pentagon, Andrews Air Force Base was immediately put on lockdown. Though Air Force One was in Florida, the feeling was that Andrews could be next on the hit list. The comings and goings of employees and family members were chaotically disrupted. I was hard at work in the "battle staff," huddled with commanders and other advisors going over contingency plans to secure the base and coordinate resources to support the Pentagon's emergency operations response. Meanwhile, my wife was frantically trying to navigate the traffic jams clogging the D.C. metropolitan area to pick up our kids, who were still stuck in school. As we scrambled to secure the base, we also had the responsibility of providing safety and refuge for the congressional representatives and other government officials who had gathered there for possible helicopter airlifts to secure locations. The atmosphere was thick with uncertainty.

***

As word started spilling out of the Pentagon that we were indeed going to war as a result of the 9/11 attacks, like all US military installations, we started preparing personnel for possible deployment to Afghanistan or other parts of the region immediately. Regardless of where they were directed to go, the troops saw this as their solemn duty. In order to make an impression that this wasn't purely an American occupation attempt, we teamed up with the

Northern Alliance and other Taliban-opposition groups to launch Operation Enduring Freedom, also known as the invasion of Afghanistan, on October 7, 2001. By December, a new interim government had been installed in the country.

After invading Afghanistan, our war posture took a sudden change in direction. I began hearing talk about contingency plans to invade Iraq and unseat Saddam Hussein. At the time, neither I nor anyone I discussed this with thought Iraq was a credible threat. We definitely hadn't heard a word about Iraq having anything to do with 9/11. Thanks to my previous assignments at the Pentagon and knowing people throughout the building and the Joint Staff, the personnel that supported the Chairman of the Joint Chiefs, I took advantage of those connections and inquired as to why we were thinking of invading Iraq. My contacts didn't have a clue, and they told me they saw no evidence that Iraq had WMD, either. Later, when we began preparing troops for deployment to Iraq, an airman asked me why we were doing this. I had no good answer. This instigated my decision to retire. As previously stated, I couldn't in good conscience send our troops off to fight a war that I couldn't justify.

***

9/11 could've been prevented if the Bush administration had listened to the CIA and the National Security Council. Richard Clarke, a counterterrorism expert, had warned Bush about the threat posed by Osama Bin Laden. But Bush and his administration weren't interested. At the December 19, 2000 "exit interview" between President Clinton and President-Elect Bush, Clinton briefed Bush on what he considered to be the nation's top five foreign policy and security concerns. First on the list: dealing with Bin Laden and Al-Qaeda. Imagine how surprised I was while watching a 2009 Sean Hannity interview with Dick Cheney, where Cheney claimed the Bush administration knew little about Al-Qaeda. I almost fell out of my chair.

In July 2001, Cofer Black, director of the CIA's Counterterrorism Center, also warned the White House of an impending attack from Bin Laden and Al-Qaeda. But Bush's team was so focused on Iraq that they had taken their eyes off our real threat. Shockingly, after the attack came to fruition two months later, the Bush administration only became even more focused on Iraq, taking advantage of 9/11 to push their agenda. Although Al-Qaeda, headquartered in Afghanistan, was responsible for 3,000 deaths on American soil, Afghanistan was merely a throughway to our government's master plan.

Though we went through the motions, I don't believe getting Bin Laden was ever really a priority for the Bush administration. In fact, during a press conference on March 13, 2002, just six months after proclaiming that he wanted Bin Laden dead or alive, Bush said, "I truly am not that concerned about him." He also said, "I really just don't spend that much time on him, to be honest with you."

***

Though we quickly removed the Taliban from power in December 2001, the Taliban didn't simply disappear. While the Bush administration focused on sending troops to Iraq, the Taliban kept surging in Afghanistan, which meant American soldiers were dying. The consequence was that by the time Bush left office, there were more US and coalition deaths in Afghanistan than there were in Iraq. ████████

██

██

██

Earlier that year, in May 2008, commanders in Afghanistan said they needed between 10,000 to 12,000 additional troops. However, word came back that they couldn't get more until we started drawing down in Iraq. Admiral Mike Mullins, the chairman of the Joint Chiefs of Staff at the time, had also called for more troops in Afghanistan, but his request was ignored. Later, in fall 2009, General Stanley McChrystal, commander of US forces in Afghanistan, said we needed up to 40,000 additional troops. The Bush administration's tunnel vision when it came to Iraq had put us in a troop deficit in Afghanistan.

The Bush administration viewed Afghanistan as a brief excursion, a preamble for the sham "War on Terror" used to legitimize invading Iraq and, later, Syria and Iran. This was all according to Donald Rumsfeld's plan, part of what I call his Middle East doctrine. Rumsfeld's philosophy was to create a diversion in order to get to the true objective.

***

Osama Bin Laden detested the United States. He hated us for our military involvement in Saudi Arabia, our continued operations in Iraq after the 1990 Desert Storm invasion, our support of Israel, and our hegemonic vision of the Middle East. You can say he declared war on us for those reasons, but he was happy to see us assail Afghanistan and Iraq.

He was ready for the fight. Bin Laden also knew that the Taliban would protect him based on *pashtunwali*, a tribal code of honor and loyalty, and not back down in its struggle against American forces. The Taliban owed Bin Laden because he had helped them confront the Soviets. Plus, there were factions that supported Bin Laden in neighboring Pakistan. They weren't going to give him up.

Bin Laden wanted to make the wars costly in order to bankrupt the United States and kill as many Americans as possible. He almost succeeded. The Bush administration originally estimated a $50 billion budget for the Iraq War. The overarching "War on Terror," which includes the invasions of Afghanistan and Iraq, have cost us an estimated $8 trillion— and the lives of more than 7,000 service members—according to Brown University's Cost of War Project. "Imagine what we could have done with that money for the American people," a retired Pentagon military official once said to me.

All this borrowed money added to our national deficit. The staggering sum also includes reconstituting our military forces, equipment, and the medical costs for treating wounded military members who suffered traumatic brain injuries, PTSD, amputations, and other life-altering medical issues. On March 4, 2009, the Pentagon announced that up to 360,000 Iraq and Afghanistan veterans may have suffered brain injuries, announcing that up to 90,000 of them will require ongoing specialized care.

Between 2007 and 2009, we experienced the Great Recession, the worst economic decline since World War II. We witnessed the effects of the Iraq War in the fallen stock market and the devaluing of the dollar, the soaring gasoline prices (the conflicts in Afghanistan and Iraq consumed more fuel than any wars in our history), a crumbling housing market, collapsing businesses, and increased unemployment. Families went deeper in debt just to survive, and our education and healthcare systems were reduced to shambles, strained in part by the thousands of veterans who will need medical care for life. Osama Bin Laden warned that he would break the United States, and he may have been right: by September 2008, our economy was on the verge of total collapse.

***

Though this mess was started by Bush, the Obama administration shouldn't escape blame for its Afghanistan policy, either. Although Obama's goal was to eventually pull out, he in fact initially did the opposite, adding more troops, as requested by the military. I feel that President Obama made a mistake by continuing the war in Afghanistan, which he called a "war of necessity." In my opinion, the Obama administration was trying to prove its strength to naysayers by taking on the Taliban. After years of rejection from the Bush administration, the generals were finally able to convince Obama that the war could be won—or at least stabilized—by sending more troops to Afghanistan. In the fall of 2009, hard-right hawks and even some conservative Democrats pressured Obama to quickly approve Gen. Stanley McChrystal's request for an additional 40,000 troops.

I find this ironic. Where were these people in the summer of 2008, when Mike Mullens was asking for more troops in Afghanistan? In May and June of that year, the Taliban killed more coalition troops in Afghanistan than the insurgents did in Iraq. In fact, we lost more troops in June 2008 than we did during the first month of the 2001 invasion. In October 2009, Dick Cheney played politics when he pressured Obama, without thinking out a new strategy or considering the consequences, to send more troops into this unmitigated disaster. Domestic politics can sometimes be our worst enemy.

Before we invaded Afghanistan, both Zbigniew Brzezinski—the former national security advisor to President Jimmy Carter—and Pervez Musharraf—the former president of Pakistan—warned of a possible quagmire. Musharraf even asked why we would start a war just to get one man. They were right: our forces remained in Afghanistan for over two decades.

It was special operations and intelligence that eventually got the leaders of Al-Qaeda. On May 2, 2011, US Navy Seals killed Bin Laden—ironically, in Pakistan, not Afghanistan. More than ten years later, on July 31, 2022, Ayman al-Zawahiri, Bin Laden's number-two in command, was killed in Kabul via a drone attack. We inflicted tremendous damage to Al-Qaeda's network, punishing them for striking our homeland. We even captured, tortured, and waterboarded Khalid Sheik Mohammed, 9/11's chief planner. I must note, however, that we didn't need a full-scale invasion or a drawn-out war to get Bin Laden. Though Afghanistan was merely the throughway to Iraq, Bush's hawks still had an agenda for the country. Their goal was to install a puppet government in Afghanistan to carry out their hegemonic occupation plans, on the backs of our military men and women. That is why they wanted to keep our troops in Afghanistan forever. Still, we accomplished our alleged original mission: we got Bin Laden, and Al-Qaeda was on the run. It was time to bring our troops home.

I fully supported President Joe Biden's withdrawal from Afghanistan. Unfortunately, though, after twenty years of American presence and continuous conflict, the Taliban once again took over Afghanistan. Yet regardless of how we feel about it, that's Afghanistan's problem, not ours. Lesson learned: you can't occupy a foreign country indefinitely and impose democracy. If the people of Afghanistan don't want the Taliban in power, they will eventually find a way to overthrow it. But it's up to them to decide who runs their government, not the United States.

CHAPTER 3

Why We Went to War

"What I find revolting is that their [the troops']
sacrifices are based on the devious deception at the
top that manipulated the system in order to satisfy
personal agendas. . . . Saddam was no threat to us."
—General Hugh Shelton, chairman of the Joint Chiefs
of Staff, as quoted in *Without Hesitation: The
Odyssey of an American Warrior*

Some people think the real reason we invaded Iraq was for Halliburton and other Bush administration–friendly companies to profit from the war. Others believed it was George W. Bush's personal vendetta for the failed assassination attempt against his father during a 1993 visit to Kuwait, commemorating the victory over Iraq in the Persian Gulf conflict.

Over the years, many military personnel I've talked to have cited access to oil as the driving motive. They weren't alone. In September 2009, Larry Wilkerson, Colin Powell's former Chief of Staff at the State Department and an outspoken critic of the Bush administration, said on a radio talk show that he thought the war was about oil or energy. Others who also followed that line of thinking were former Federal Reserve Chairman Alan Greenspan and MSNBC's Rachel Maddow, who discussed that topic in her documentary *Why We Did It*. Though oil was discussed as a benefit, it was never a primary reason for the invasion.[1,2] I think Madeleine Albright summed

it up best for me: "we took our eye off the ball in Afghanistan to invade Iraq for God-only-knows reasons."

Gen. Hugh Shelton, the top military officer in the US Armed Forces and the principal military advisor to the president and the secretary of defense, said that Iraq wasn't a threat to the United States. Shelton is an honorable, trustworthy man who loved the troops. He periodically invited me and the other senior leaders of the Combatant Joint Commands to the Pentagon, to brief and update him on enlisted issues. During one of those meetings, Shelton expressed his desire to secure his own personal senior enlisted advisor, just like the combatant commanders and service chiefs (the four-star heads of the Navy, Army, Air Force, and Marine Corps). He sought our opinion. As the top uniformed military officer in the Department of Defense, Shelton thought it was important for him to hear about the issues directly from his own senior enlisted confidante. I left that meeting convinced of his admiration for the enlisted corps. I'm

not surprised, then, that Shelton didn't support the Bush administration's lies which were going to put the troops in harm's way. Sadly, we now know the invasion of Iraq was not about WMD either. In fact, whether Iraq had WMD or not, we were going in. Also, even if there was a coup against Saddam, we would still invade and put in a government of our choice.

The truth is that our troops were sent to Iraq based on the hegemonic ambitions of a radical faction within the Bush administration. There are three specific reasons why we started the war.

The first reason was ideological, to restore the United States "credibility" and standing as the world's only super-power. The invasion of Iraq was the culmination of a long-simmering plan to reshape the Middle East—and the world. This plan was hatched by Donald Rumsfeld; Deputy Secretary of Defense Paul Wolfowitz; Under Secretary of Defense Douglas Feith; and Chairman of the Defense Policy Board Richard Perle. Their agenda originated with the Project for the New American Century (PNAC), a now-defunct neoconservative think tank focused on implementing our foreign policy through the use of force. The PNAC advocated for unilateralism and preemptive military action to suppress any potential threats and prevent other countries from rising to superpower status. Simply put, the PNAC craved American world dominance.

In the 1990s, yielding to pressure from the PNAC, the Clinton administration introduced a policy for regime change in Iraq, but this policy was never carried out. In fact, Clinton had no intention of invading Iraq—the policy was only to appease the PNAC and other hawkish groups. Later, when Bush came to power, some of his advisors complained that Clinton's inaction made the United States appear weak. They believed we had to get rid of Saddam to assert our dominance. If you were to look back at transcripts or watch videos of key Bush officials in the time before 9/11, you will notice a lot of talk about our credibility being at stake, and the need to strengthen it.[3]

As I pored over thousands of documents, a clear picture emerged: Rumsfeld and Wolfowitz were obsessed with restoring the United States' credibility. Rumsfeld, in particular, was deeply concerned about our inability to bring peace to the Middle East. But he wasn't especially interested in spreading democracy, as some in the Bush administration—

---

3 An early example of this thinking was a memo from Rumsfeld to Condoleezza Rice stating that "A major success in Iraq would enhance US credibility and influence throughout the region. If Saddam's regime were ousted, we would have a much-improved position in the region and elsewhere." ("Iraq" July 27, 2001) Nothing was said about our national security or the common defense of the United States, only our credibility. Throughout my analysis of thousands of Iraq War policy documents, the United States' credibility was the driving force of our foreign policy. The Bush administration even pressured the United Nations to act by saying its credibility was at stake. In his book *Decision Points*, President Bush writes: "I would remind the UN that Saddam's defiance was a threat to the credibility of the institute." (*Decision Points*, page XX) In Doug Feith's own words: "Success in Iraq would also demonstrate that the United States is capable of preserving a costly effort to defend its interests. This would increase American credibility, making it easier in the future to win cooperation from other countries." (*War and Decision*, page 523). I assume "a costly effort" was the blood of our military men and women for the Bush administration's personal political goals and agenda.

including Bush himself—aspired to do. What he truly craved was power and influence.

For example, on July 27, 2001, Rumsfeld sent a memo to National Security Advisor Condoleezza Rice titled "Iraq." The memo stated that "A major success in Iraq would enhance U.S. credibility and influence throughout the region. If Saddam's regime were ousted, we would have a much-improved position in the region and elsewhere." Rumsfeld says nothing here about our national security, only emphasizing "credibility."

The Bush administration even pressured the United Nations to act using the same argument. In his book *Decision Points,* Bush wrote: "I would remind the UN that Saddam's defiance was a threat to the credibility of the institute." Meanwhile, Doug Feith, in his book, *War and Decision,* said that "Success in Iraq would also demonstrate that the United States is capable of persevering a costly effort to defend its interests. This would increase American credibility, making it easier in the future to win cooperation from other countries."

I assume the "costly effort" refers to the blood our service members spilled for the Bush administration's political agenda. The administration gambled with the lives of our military members, sending them off to fight for American credibility, not in defense of our country.

***

Donald Rumsfeld and his cronies felt that the United States lacked the resolve to broker peace in the Middle East. They mentioned past incidents where, in their opinion, we ran from the fight: the withdrawal from Vietnam, leaving Lebanon after one of our barracks was bombed in Beirut; and the retreat from Mogadishu in Somalia where we pulled our forces out after dead Americans were dragged through the streets. The hawks argued that in the past, when things got tough, we simply ran away. In their minds, this encouraged more acts of terrorism and aggression against the United States.

According to Doug Feith's book, Rumsfeld said that "U.S. weakness in the face of Saddam's aggressiveness undercuts our leverage in the region on everything, including in the Israeli-Palestinian diplomacy." This was in response to a debate between the State Department and the Department of Defense about invading Iraq. Another example is a note Paul Wolfowitz sent Rumsfeld on October 22, 2002: "Middle Easterners despise fear. To do nothing amounts in Middle Easterners' eyes as surrender."

Invading Afghanistan would prove to the world once and for all that we weren't cowards who would back down after being injured. Our decision to attack Al-Qaeda and the Taliban was encouraged at home and abroad because everyone understood that, following 9/11, the United States had a right to retaliate. After the perceived success in Afghanistan, Rumsfeld and his neocons decided the time was right for the next strategic step: using 9/11 to justify invading Iraq.

***

After leaving the DRT in 2008, I went to work for the Office of Policy Planning in the Office of the Under Secretary of

Defense. There, I read a study called "Blunders in Military and Foreign Strategy" by Zachary Shore, a history professor at the Naval Postgraduate School in Monterey, California, who specializes in international conflict. At the time, Shore was hoping the Pentagon would fund his study, but the Pentagon turned him down. In retrospect, I can see why, as the study reveals some uncomfortable truths that hit too close to home.

In his study, Shore examined the thought patterns of individual decision-makers. In particular, patterns that created obstacles to establishing prudent policies. Shore called these patterns "cognition traps," meaning the rigid mindsets formed from faulty reason. He termed one of these traps "exposure anxiety," the fear of being exposed as weak. In my opinion, this "exposure anxiety" is exactly what Dick Cheney and Donald Rumsfeld suffered from.[4]

Shore mentioned something else that struck me. He said that when hawkish countries bungle up their military interventions, their knee-jerk response is to squander resources— setting back progress, prosperity, security, and strength. In March 2013, Stewart Bowen, the Special Inspector General for Iraq Reconstruction, released a report to Congress stat-

---

4   Per Doug Feith's *War and Decision* (page 209), in response to a debate between the State Department and the Department of Defense on invading Iraq, Rumsfeld said: "U.S. weakness in the face of Saddam's aggressiveness undercuts our leverage in the region on everything, including in the Israeli-Palestinian diplomacy." ████████

ing that by that point, the US government had spent more than $60 billion in Iraq with very little to show for it. We now know the Iraq War squandered more than $1 trillion dollars and cost the lives of more than 4,500 American service members.

***

The second reason why we invaded Iraq was to start a proxy war on behalf of Israel by eliminating its enemies, Hamas and Hezbollah.

Although Hamas and Hezbollah were the Bush administration's true targets, we couldn't go after them directly, as their cells were embedded within their communities while working on the ground resisting Israeli aggression. Newt Gingrich, who was a former Defense Policy Board member and an advisor to Rumsfeld, provided a study paper to Rumsfeld titled "Newt Gingrich's Seven Strategic Necessities." The paper offered what Gingrich called some "current assumptions" regarding the issue of Hamas: "Palestine may present us the challenge of trying to win a total war against an enemy hiding among civilians. Hamas leaders state publicly that not a single Jew will be left and that not a single meter of territory will be left in Jewish hands. This is a declaration of total war." Gingrich also stated that "We know how to fight a war against a nation. However, we have no doctrine to fight against forces that could hide out among the people."

Benjamin Netanyahu has always wanted to take Hamas on in Gaza with street-to-street, house-to-house fighting, regardless of the loss of innocent Palestinians. However, we would not give them the green light because Israel or the US would not be able to overcome the outrage of the international community.

Rumsfeld and Paul Wolfowitz had the answer: go after the so-called state sponsors of terrorism, namely Iraq, Syria, and Iran.

A cabal headed by Rumsfeld, Wolfowitz, Richard Perle, Doug Feith, and Gingrich formulated a strategy to crush Hamas's and Hezbollah's military and financial support networks in Iraq, Syria, and Iran. Rumsfeld and Wolfowitz believed that these groups' hostilities toward Israel prevented peace between Israel and Palestine. A memo Feith prepared for Rumsfeld to send to Condolezza Rice noted, "in order to have peace we must change the status quo of the culture and the leaders." Basically, they wanted to destroy Hamas and Hezbollah by dissolving the governments that backed them.[5]

---

5   ██
    ██
    ██
    ████████████████████████████████ ("FYI,"
"Middle East: Talking Points") In an op-ed for the *Wall Street Journal*, John Bolton wrote: "Changing Tehran's regime could eliminate its continuing financing of and weapons supplies for Hamas and Hezbollah." In his book, *End Game*, Air Force Lt. Gen. (Ret.) Thomas McInerney, a supporter of the rush to war, stated: "Our visit to Israel in July 2003, organized by the America-Israel Friendship League, has been critical to our understanding of why the 'roadmap to peace' will not succeed unless Iran, Syria, and Saudi Arabia stop funding terror. As long as Hamas, Hezbollah, and other major terrorist groups are funded and led from this Web of Terror, peace is impossible."

Neither Hamas or Hezbollah recognize Israel's legitimacy. Hamas was created in 1987 with a charter calling for the destruction of Israel and replacing it with an Islamic Palestinian state. Hezbollah is a Lebanese group that wants to eradicate all Western influence from Lebanon by establishing an Islamic government. Its early goal was to end Israel's occupation of southern Lebanon. Both Hamas and Hezbollah view themselves as resistance movements rather than terrorist networks. Our objective was to diminish the Palestinians' hopes for creating a state of their own unless they made peace with Israel on Israel's terms, or remained in occupation under the control of Israel. In order to do that, we had to vanquish Hamas and Hezbollah by invading Iraq, which financed these two groups.[6]

---

6 ████████████████████████████████████
████████████████████████

The documents I found that discussed going on the offensive for Israel surprised me. I understood that Israel was our ally, but I couldn't comprehend why some officials felt the need to initiate a war on behalf of another country—a war that could negatively affect our national security and set the Middle East on fire. Why were we invading Iraq on behalf of Israel? How was Israel driving our foreign policy in the Middle East?

Many of our elected officials, including members of Congress, are highly influenced by the pro-Israel lobby, of which American Israel Public Affairs Committee (AIPAC) is the largest and most powerful. On its website it states: **"WE STAND** with those who stand with Israel. The AIPAC PAC is a bipartisan, pro-Israel political action committee. It is the largest pro-Israel PAC in America and contributed more resources directly to candidates than any other PAC. **98% of AIPAC-backed candidates won their general election races in 2022." "We base our support only on a candidate's support for the U.S.-Israel relationship."** Doug Feith, for instance, is an unabashed supporter of Israel: "Pro-Israel organizations have long been active in American politics," he noted in a November 2011 *Wall Street Journal* piece that he wrote called "Israel Should Be a U.S. Campaign Issue." The Israel lobby has "helped ensure that candidates' attitudes toward Israel would be an important

element in congressional and presidential elections," Feith explained. He then gave an example for how pro-Israel groups "exerted themselves" to successfully defeat the 1984 reelection of Charles Percy, a Republican senator from Illinois and chairman of the Senate Foreign Relations Committee, who was slammed for saying that the United States should engage with the Palestine Liberation Organization. Feith finished his piece with a threat to the president: "Mr. Obama can expect to pay a substantial political price in 2012 for his antagonism toward Israel and feckless courting of its enemies."

The Jewish Institute for National Security Affairs (JINSA) helped shape Feith's ideology. JINSA is a think tank that rejects the creation of a sovereign Palestinian state and advocates for regime change in countries that back what it regards as terrorist groups that threaten Israel—countries such as Iraq, Iran, and Syria.[7]

In recent years, the political influence of the Israel lobby has manifested during the debate over the Iran nuclear deal. Officially known as the Joint Comprehensive Plan of Action (JCPOA), the deal was an agreement made in 2015 between the five permanent members of the United Nations Security Council—China, France, Russia, the United Kingdom, and the United States—and Germany (P5+1). Per the deal, Iran would eliminate its enriched uranium stockpile

---

7   JINSA Report Number 868, March 11, 2009: "JINSA is an unabashed supporter of the State of Israel." The policy of eradicating the countries that allegedly supported Hamas and Hezbollah is derived from JINSA's goal of "security at all costs for Israel."

and halt the development of its alleged nuclear weapons program in exchange for relief from UN and US sanctions. I myself thought the deal was a win-win for all parties. Yet, Israel and its supporters demanded more concessions from Iran. They also wanted the Iranians to limit their ballistic missile program. Iran flatly refused, fearing these concessions would put its security at risk from Israel and the United States. This was probably a prudent calculation on Iran's part, considering the past invasions of Afghanistan and Iraq.

Nearly two years before the JCPOA, senators Robert Menendez and Mark Kirk introduced the Nuclear Weapon Free Iran Act, which stated that if Israel should decide to attack Iran as "self-defense" against Iran's nuclear weapons program, then the United States must provide Israel with military and economic support. The goal was to derail the nuclear deal. In January 2015, Speaker of the House John Boehner went behind President Obama's back when he invited Israeli Prime Minister Benjamin Netanyahu—who has been lying about the threat of Iran's nuclear program for years—to address Congress in an effort to convince the United States to side with Israel's policy toward Iran over Obama's. Later that same year, as the JCPOA negotiations were being finalized, pro-Israel lobbyists recruited Senator Tom Cotton to convince forty-seven of his colleagues to publicly side with Netanyahu, saying they refused to honor the deal brokered by their own president. However, the Israeli supporters and lobbyists didn't prevail. The deal was agreed upon by Iran and the P5+1. However, Trump pulled out of the deal in 2018 and there's currently an all-out push to keep the Biden administration from entering into a new deal with Iran.

Prior to George W. Bush, American presidential administrations had attempted to negotiate peace to the Middle East through diplomacy. The crowning achievement was the 1978 Camp David Accords, which brokered a historic treaty between Israel and Egypt. However, from the documents I analyzed, Bush's advisors felt diplomatic negotiations wouldn't be possible because Hezbollah and Hamas had called for the destruction of Israel. The hawks believed we needed to go to war with Iraq. In their minds, the United States looked weak by not pursuing Hamas and Hezbollah. But, as stated earlier, we couldn't go after them directly. If we did, it would be no secret that we were fighting on behalf of Israel. So Bush's advisors had to come up with a different pretext.[8]

Israel is an ally of the United States, and we should help defend it, but only if it is legitimately invaded. That's why I have a problem saying the United States should have an

---

8   Newt Gingrich, a former defense policy board member and advisor to Donald Rumsfeld, provided Rumsfeld a study paper offering what he called some "current assumptions" to the issue of Hamas. Gingrich wrote: "Palestine may present us the challenge of trying to win a total war against an enemy hiding among civilians. Hamas leaders state publicly that not a single Jew will be left and that not a single meter of territory will be left in Jewish hands. This is a declaration of total war" ("Newt Gingrich's Seven Strategic Necessities," June 27, 2003). Gingrich also stated: "We know how to fight a war against a nation. However, we have no doctrine to fight against forces that could hide out among the people." Rumsfeld and Wolfowitz's answer: go after the so-called state sponsors of terrorism: Iraq, Syria, and Iran.

unbreakable, unquestionable bond with Israel. How can one broker peace between two parties if one party—in this case, the Palestinians—perceives that you favor the other? Moreover, the $3.7 billion a year we give Israel in military aid is no incentive to make peace with the Palestinians. Instead, this blank check sends a message that the United States is willing to support Israel no matter what. If we're going to get involved in the Middle East peace process, we should be open to hearing all sides. If we don't have a more balanced view, we can't help either Israel or Palestine in the long run.

***

The third reason we invaded Iraq was to bring democracy to the Middle East through force. To justify this attack on a sovereign nation, the case was first made that Iraq possessed WMD. However, after no WMD were found, Bush changed his tune around Saddam's threat to the United States. He talked more about freedom for the Iraqi people and democracy. Doug Feith believed that Bush's open talk of Middle Eastern democracy was "off-message." Feith also believed the president's words would give ammunition to his critics, who had always maintained that the Iraq War was never about WMD[9] and that the desire for democracy couldn't justify going to war.

---

9   Doug Feith: "The president no longer cited Saddam's record or the threats from the Baathist regime as reasons for going to war; rather, he focused almost exclusively on the aim of promoting democracy" (*War and Decision*, p. 521).

If we hadn't gotten bogged down in Iraq, the plan was to invade Syria next, then Iran. In fact, Israelis working with the Bush administration wanted us to go after Syria and, in particular, Iran before pursuing Iraq. They saw Iran and Syria as the main sponsors of Hamas and Hezbollah, and thus a bigger threat to Israel than Saddam Hussein. However, the American hawks decided to attack Iraq first. In their mind, there was a stronger case for attacking Iraq. After all, the invasion of Iraq couldn't be perceived as executed on behalf of Israel—it could be positioned as necessary for the United States' national defense following 9/11.[10]

So, who exactly were these war hawks advising the president, eager to lead us down a path of destruction?

---

10 ██
██
████████████████████████

CHAPTER 4

The Neocons

"Neoconservatives have the president's ear. Bush has embraced so much of what we believe."
— Joshua Muravchik, resident scholar at the American Enterprise Institute in "How to Save the Neocons," an open letter dated October 31, 2006

The neoconservatives, or neocons, were thus named by lifelong conservatives during the Reagan years. They were former Democrats who broke ranks and aligned themselves with Ronald Regan's ideology of American exceptionalism and staunch anti-communism. This extremely militaristic faction of the Republican Party was also responsible for shaping foreign policy during the two Bush administrations. After the collapse of the Soviet Union, their focus shifted from fighting communism to eradicating so-called "Islamic terrorism." The neocons got us into Iraq, and they've been trying to get the United States to invade Syria and remove its president, Bashar al-Assad. They've also led the charge to disrupt the Iran nuclear deal and are culpable for our strained relationship with Russia, which I'll discuss later.

The neocons advocate for unilateralism and preemptive military action to suppress potential foreign threats and prevent any other nations from rising to superpower status. They want world dominance. American imperialism and hegemony in the Middle East is one of their major goals. The attack on Iraq was the first stage of this plan.

As Americans, we must ask, how did these people take over our government? How did they get us into a quagmire that could go down in history as the worst foreign policy blunder the United States has ever made? The neocons guided President George W. Bush into launching an attack that ultimately led to a civil war between the Shiites and the

Sunnis in Iraq, destabilizing the Middle East even further and giving birth to the militant Islamic State (IS).

The American Enterprise Institute (AEI), the premier neocon think tank, counted Dick Cheney as a former Senior Fellow. When he was chosen to lead President George W. Bush's transition team, he surrounded Bush with fellow AEI members, placing them in key positions: Scooter Libby, Elliot Abrams, Donald Rumsfeld, Paul Wolfowitz, Richard Perle, Newt Gingrich, Doug Feith, Peter Rodman, and Abe Shulsky, who was to Feith what Karl Rove was to Bush, the strategizing brain behind many of Feith's manipulative talking points. In fact, approximately twenty members of Bush's cabinet came from AEI, something that Bush bragged about in two speeches, one in February 2003, the other in February 2007. At the State Department, John Bolton was the inside man assigned to advance the neocons' agenda. He also kept his eye on the only "outsider" to hold a key foreign policy position, Secretary of State Colin Powell.

Although President Bush should be held accountable for his role in the Iraq War, he was misled by the neocons just like the rest of us. They convinced Bush he could achieve his goals by following their roadmap. There's no doubt Bush knows that the neocons betrayed him, and I'm sure that's why he has remained tight-lipped about the Iraq War since leaving office. He did make a telling Freudian slip on May 18, 2022, at his presidential center at Southern Methodist University in Texas. While condemning Vladimir Putin's attack on Ukraine, Bush inadvertently decried "the decision of one man to launch a wholly unjustified and brutal invasion of Iraq."

In November 2001, I had the opportunity to spend some time with President Bush and the First Lady on an Air Force One mission to visit some troops that were preparing for deployment to Afghanistan. I must admit that I really like Bush as a person. He has a great sense of humor, but he can also be focused and businesslike when necessary. However, I blame him for not taking action as soon as he saw how his advisors had misled him. The neocons took the president's agenda and twisted it to their advantage, drafting policy that fulfilled their ambitions by distorting Bush's sincere wish for Middle Eastern democracy.[1]

Bush should've made changes in his administration as soon as he realized what some of his advisors were doing. Even after some were forced to resign, they were able to remain in the administration in other capacities. For instance, two of Doug Feith's former key deputies during the run up to the war, J. D. Crouch—the former assistant secretary of defense for international security policy and deputy national security advisor at the White House—and Peter Rodman— the former assistant secretary of defense for International

---

[1]   In 2002, Karen Kwiatkowski, a retired Air Force Lieutenant Colonel, tried to warn us about the neocons in a series of anonymous papers she authored titled "Insider Notes from the Pentagon." One of her warning notes: "I came to share with many NSA colleagues a kind of unease, a sense that something was awry. What seemed out of place was the strong and open pro-Israel and anti-Arab orientation in an ostensibly apolitical policy-generation staff within the Pentagon."

Security Assistance—became members of the Defense Policy Board, which advises the secretary of defense. Worse still, Paul Wolfowitz was hired as a key advisor at the State Department after leaving the Pentagon and being forced to leave the top leadership post at the World Bank. Both Wolfowitz and Crouch worked on a rejected 1992 draft of the Defense Planning Guidance, which recommended a United States preemptive war strategy to influence the world.

***

The neocons have learned nothing from the disastrous invasions of Afghanistan and Iraq. In fact, they will attempt to do it again. In October of 2006, unabashed neocon Joshua Muravchik of AEI wrote a think piece called "Operation Comeback: How to Save the Neocons." In it, he brags about how the "intellectual" contributions of the neocons helped defeat communism and will help vanquish jihadism. Muravchik also said the neocons must sharpen their game and continue the fight. Echoing John Bolton, Muravchik demanded that Bush bomb Iran. He also thought that if we didn't do it for them, Israel would bomb Iran. We also learned in August 2015, through a leaked audio recording, that Benjamin Netanyahu and Ehud Barak, Israel's former defense minister, indeed planned to bomb Iran in 2010, 2011, and 2012, but complications prevented them each time.

What really got my attention was Muravchik's recommendation to recruit Joe Lieberman, the former senator from Connecticut. He felt that the neocons needed elected leaders who were sympathetic to their cause. He said that

Senator John McCain and former New York City mayor Rudy Giuliani were both persuadable. Both McCain and Giuliani were 2008 presidential candidates. Before Giuliani dropped out, he had a team of neocons advising him. And as soon as McCain became the presumptive Republican nominee, the neocons ran toward him.

McCain's foreign policy and security advisor was Randy Scheunemann, former co-director for the Project for the New American Century, who pushed for war with Iraq and has strong ties to the neocon movement. And guess who McCain's number-one supporter was, after his wife and after Senator Lindsey Graham of South Carolina? None other than Joe Lieberman, who had campaigned for McCain and traveled to the Middle East with him. Lieberman was a Democrat until he lost his reelection bid during the primaries over his steadfast support for the Iraq War. When that happened, Lieberman ran as an Independent, with the support of the Republican Party, and won. In fact it was rumored that Lieberman was McCain's top choice to be his running mate until Sarah Palin entered the picture.

Since the neocons couldn't convince Bush to bomb Iran, they latched on to John McCain. Who knows what McCain would have done if he became president?

***

I paid close attention to the 2016 presidential campaign, taking notice of which candidates the neocons supported. During the September 16, 2015, Republican presidential debate, the blatant appeasement to Israel and its lobbying machine was so relentless that even conservative commentator Ann

Coulter lashed out at the pandering of the candidates. As we now know, the neocons ended up with Donald Trump, who publicly said the invasion of Iraq was "dumb." Still, the neocons believed they could get Trump's ear, since he also felt that the Iran nuclear deal was "weak." At first, they tried to secure John Bolton as secretary of state. After that didn't work out, they eventually got him a position as the President's national security advisor. The neocons did get a big win from Trump: he withdrew from the Iran nuclear deal.

The neocons believe that we still have unfinished business in Syria and Iran. President Obama gave them the rhetoric to go after Assad, the president of Syria. During a March 20, 2013 joint press conference with Israel's Prime Minister Benjamin Netanyahu, Obama made the mistake of saying Assad "must go." The neocons jumped on his statement. They tried but failed to get President Obama to take out Assad. When he refused, the neocons accused Obama of weakness because he didn't topple Syria's government. The hawks pressured Obama to attack Syria because they believed his credibility was on the line, despite the fact that our national security wasn't at risk. The neocons were almost able to sway Obama with the same exposure anxiety they used to push the Iraq War. Luckily, unlike Bush, Obama didn't fall into the trap. In fact, he went on record saying he was proud that he stuck to his guns. "The perception was that my credibility was at stake; that America's credibility was at stake. And so, for me to press the pause button at that moment, I knew, would cost me politically," Obama told *The Atlantic* in 2016, adding, "And the fact that I was able to pull back from the immediate pressures and think through in my own mind what was in America's interest, not only with respect to Syria but also with respect to our democracy, was as tough a decision as I've made."[2]

***

The neocons are still on the prowl and still planning a comeback. If we allow them back into our government, if we enable them to once again exert their influence on our foreign policy, this could lead to a larger arms race with China and Russia, and possibly World War III. The neocons are plotting to keep President Biden from entering into a new nuclear deal with Iran unless Iran succumbs to Israel's demands. And if there's no new deal, then the neocons and Israel will ultimately get the war they want. "Words will not stop them, Mr. President," former Israeli prime minister Yair Lapid told Biden in July 2022, speaking about Iran. "Diplomacy will not stop them. The only way to stop them is to put a credible military threat on the table."

---

2   Obama said there was a militarized foreign policy playbook in Washington that is a trap that can lead to bad decisions (see Jeffrey Goldberg, "The Obama Doctrine" *The Atlantic*, April 2016, https://www. theatlantic.com/magazine/archive/2016/04/the-obama-doctrine/471525/.)

CHAPTER 5

The Plan and Strategy to Go to War (How They Did It)

"I said, 'Are we still going to war with Iraq?' And he said, 'Oh, it is worse than that! I just got this down from upstairs from the Secretary of Defense's Office today. This is a memo that describes how we are going to take out seven countries in five years, starting with Iraq, then Syria and Lebanon, then finishing off with Iran.'"

—General Wesley Clark, former Supreme Allied Commander, Europe and US European Command, sharing a conversation he had with a senior officer in the Pentagon in the weeks following 9/11, during an interview with *Democracy Now!* on March 2, 2007

The Iraq War was part of the neocon plan to dominate the Middle East in support of Israel. As mentioned earlier, although Iraq was the starting point, Israel originally wanted us to invade Syria or Iran first, as Israel felt that these countries were the biggest supporters of Hezbollah and Hamas.[1]

███████████████████████████████████████

███████████████████████████████████████

███████████████████████████████████████

███████████████████████████████████████

███████████████████████████████████████

Before 9/11, the most hawkish neocons in the Pentagon had made up their minds they were going after Saddam as the first phase of the strategy. It was felt the U.S. needed to challenge and get Saddam out of the way to show strength and influence in the region. They felt previous Administrations were weak and the United Nations was ineffective and had no credibility. The U.S. had a policy of Regime Change implemented during the Clinton Administration, yet Saddam was still in power. So they decided to they show the world that the U.S. "meant what it said and said what it meant."

1   Per comments made by John Bolton in February 2003, once regime change plans in Iraq were completed, it will be necessary to deal with the "so-called threats" from Syria, Iran, and North Korea afterward ("Foreign Policy in Focus," February 20, 2003).

2   "Presentation—The case for Action," September 12, 2002, spelled out why the neocons chose to go after Iraq first.

The neocons desperately tried to come up with a pretext for attacking Iraq. They felt American support waning among the Arab nations that loathed Saddam, such as Saudi Arabia and Kuwait. This weakened our position with the Palestinians. 9/11 gave them justification.[3]

Immediately after 9/11, the neocons went into overdrive, telegraphing the message that we had to invade Iraq, on the unfounded premise that Saddam possessed WMD. They claimed that if Saddam were stockpiling nuclear weapons, then he would use them to intimidate neighboring countries, which would limit American influence in the region. This strategy was based on the anticipatory self-defense doctrine, a preemptive offensive tactic borrowed from the Israelis.

If the Iraq invasion had gone smoothly, the neocons would have immediately begun the Syrian phase of their campaign.[4] In order to "prepare the battlefield," Rumsfeld's team was ready to accuse Syria of aiding Iraq. Though Syria, like Iraq, posed no immediate threat to our national defense, the neocons began sowing fear, hinting that Syria possessed chemical weapons and sponsored terrorism.

As for Iran, the neocons believed that it would be hard to invade it under the pretense of "liberation." Unlike Iraq, Iran did in fact have a participatory political system, though repressive and incomplete. So they went with another tac-

---

3   "We must get a policy for Iraq settled fast." (Memo from Rumsfeld to the State Department, "Iraq," September 5, 2001).

4   [redacted]

tic, trying to destabilize Iran by promoting an uprising, both with internal support (particularly among young people, women, and journalists) and with the help of exiled Iranians. That uprising eventually came to fruition in the summer of 2009. However, by then the Obama administration wanted no part of another war in the Middle East and so it stayed out of Iran's business. The hawks were furious.

***

They decided Saddam having WMD was a threat to our National Security. Though Saddam may not have directly used WMD against us, terrorists getting their hands on them could use them against us and not be attributed to Saddam.

The neocons now had a locked plan in place that they believed the American public would buy.[5]

---

5   Memo: Hadley Small Group Discussion on Iraq, "A casus belli for action," February 11, 2002. With the newly declared War on Terror in place and 9/11 still fresh on the minds of Americans, the neocons discussed using Iraq's violations of United Nations Security Council Resolution (UNSCR) 687 and its link to terrorism as major arguments in making the case for war. ██
██
██
██
██
██
██
██
██
██Although there was never any link, the neocons refused to give it up. ██████████████
████████████████████████
██████████████████████ "On August 14, give Tina Shelton brief on Iraq/ Al-Qaeda to McLaughlin (CIA)." Shelton was an intelligence analyst on loan from DIA and working for the hawks in the Pentagon's Special Intelligence Office. Another former member was Congressman Chris Carney, Democrat from Pennsylvania, an intelligence analyst under Doug Feith. Back in 2006, as a newly elected congressman, when asked about a congressional investigation of prewar intelligence, Mr. Carney said "Let's win the war first, then maybe look at how we got into it." However, as of this date he has

***

After the neocons cemented their strategy, the next step was to get Congress on board. This was achieved through political pressure.[6] Congressional leaders, in particular Republicans, were forced to vote in favor of military action before the upcoming recess. A few top Republicans, such as Texas Congressman Dick Armey, were reluctant at first, but were eventually strong-armed into supporting the resolution. Bush's advisors told them they had no choice but to stand behind their president. House Speaker Dennis Hastert and Senate Leader Trent Lott also fell in line, choosing party loyalty over the good of the country. One Republican, Nebraska Senator Chuck Hagel (later secretary of defense in the Obama administration) was branded a traitor for daring to voice concern over going to war. Meanwhile, the Democrats were afraid of being perceived as weak on defense. Exploiting this fear to their advantage, the Bush administration threatened to use "weakness" to discredit the Democrats during the 2002 midterm campaign season. Some Democrats with

---

not talked about his contribution and the reason we invaded Iraq. Another August 2002 memo ███████████

██

Notes," August 20, 2002). ███████ a memorandum from Shelton saying that she was upset because DIA refused to cooperate on finding the alleged link between Al-Qaeda and Iraq. Scooter Libby thought finding a link would be useful. He preferred WMD as "rationale" to go to war.

6   ███████████████████████████████████████

██

██

███████████████████████████

presidential aspirations, such as Joe Biden, John Kerry, and Hillary Clinton, caved in, voting for war.

The neocons also convinced Congress that the war resolution would strengthen the president's hand as far as working with the UN. After all, they had warned the UN that Iraq had flouted the will of the Security Council for more than a decade. If the UN remained reluctant to address Iraq, the neocons argued, then the United States would have no choice but to act alone.[7] Finally, on October 2, 2002, Congress authorized President Bush to invade Iraq.[8]

A crucial aspect of the first draft of the resolution that Bush sent to Congress was an authorization allowing the president to order troops anywhere in the Middle East for other military confrontations. In fact, when Congress gave the Bush administration the green light to invade Iraq, it was

---

7   ███████████████████████████████████
    ███████████████████████████████████
    ███████████████████████████████████

8   Even though the Bush administration wanted this resolution, they
    had made up their mind that if they did not get the resolution,
    they could still act legally without it. ███████████████████
    ███████████████████████████████████
    ███████████████████████████████████
    ███████████████████████████████████
    ███████████████████ Between the brains and nerve center at the
    Pentagon and in Cheney's office and White House legal counsel
    Alberto Gonzalez, the president was convinced that he did not need
    congressional approval or UN support to defend the nation due to
    "anticipatory self-defense." They were going to war regardless, but
    preferred congressional cover. The neocons pressured Congress and
    the world with a theme of "with us are against us."

also permitting it to use force in Syria and Iran, and anywhere else the administration perceived threats.

***

Now that the invasion had been authorized, the only thing left were the UN inspections. Bush's hawks didn't want these inspections to work.[9] In fact, while waiting for the results of the December 2002 Iraq Declaration (Iraq's reports to the UN concerning WMD), the neocons furiously prepared talking points to undermine it. They hoped that Saddam would maintain his claim that he had no WMD, as they were eager to go on the offensive and say that Saddam was lying, despite a lack of concrete proof. The important thing for the neocons was to convince the UN, come hell or high water—just as they had convinced Congress and the American people—that Saddam Hussein was a serious threat that had to be deposed for the good of the world.[10]

---

9   "If we allow the UN MOVIC [Monitoring, Verification and Inspection Commission] more time which could take up to a year, our credibility would be damaged. Time is not on our side."

10

This is why the Bush administration did everything it could to undermine Hans Blix, head of the United Nations Monitoring, Verification and Inspection Commission. During the final planning stages of the invasion, Blix told the UN Security Council that Iraq was actually cooperating with his inspectors. That, of course, didn't sit well with the neocons. They were concerned that Blix's report would screw up their plan. ████████████████████████████████

██

██

example, the United States wanted its own armed inspection team to go anywhere in Iraq, at any time. Blix refused, and the neocons knew that Saddam would reject these demands as well.

Mohamed El-Bardai, director general of the International Atomic Energy Agency, also stood in the way of the neocons. El-Bardai found nothing to confirm the supposition that Iraq had an active nuclear program. Therefore the neocons tried to undermine him, too. In March 2003, a week before the start of the war, Vice President Cheney began a smear campaign, calling El-Bardai incompetent.

The Bush administration was dead set on discounting anyone who stood in the way of their cause. Along with US congressional representatives and UN officials, the neocons went after Cabinet members, such as Secretary of State Colin Powell, whom they didn't consider a "team player." Rumsfeld and Dick Cheney worked behind Powell's back, sending numerous notes to the White House without alerting the State Department. As mentioned earlier, John Bolton was keeping his eye on Powell at the State Department, on behalf of the Pentagon hawks. Doug Feith openly bragged that he and his cronies had more influence over the president than Colin Powell and the State Department. Powell worked tirelessly to make the neocons think twice about what they were doing. He advocated for a diplomatic solution, but Rumsfeld, Wolfowitz, and Feith rebuked his attempts for peaceful UN resolutions.[11]

Another strategy the neocons employed was creating the false impression that they were actually making reasonable attempts to preempt conflict by offering Saddam the chance to go into exile.[12] They proposed that Saddam escape to Chile or Japan, as these countries were far away, politically stable, and had no significant population of pro-Saddam sympathizers. Basically, they wanted to place Saddam under house arrest and force him to give up his wealth, insisting that he

survive on an allowance of a few thousand dollars a month. The neocons knew that Saddam wouldn't accept such a ridiculous deal. His refusal to go into exile would leave the United States with no choice but to depose him via force.

***

Bush's hawks were also keen on tapping into Iraq's opposition forces in order to give the invasion legitimacy. They wanted to make it seem as though the invasion was a liberation effort instigated by the Iraqis themselves, and that the United States was only there to help.[13] Furthermore, the Bush administration wanted to use the opposition for rear-end area missions and security, to help suppress any civil unrest after Saddam was gone.

One of these opposition groups was the Iraqi National Congress (INC), led by Ahmed Chalabi. Chalabi was a secular Shiite from a prominent Iraqi political family who had built solid relationships with Turkey, Iran, and the United States. The neocons saw him as the person most capable of handling Iraq's various opposition groups. For Chalabi, collaborating with the Americans was a chance to get revenge on Saddam, whom he believed was responsible for filing charges against him in Jordan that resulted in the loss of his family's banking business. However, the INC fed us faulty intel about the existence of WMD: out of five sources put forth by the INC, only one was deemed reliable, two

13 ███████████████████████████████
    ███████████████████████████████

were deemed of little importance, and two were considered worthless.

The CIA and the State Department didn't trust Chalabi, but some people in the Department of Defense were sold on him. Perle, Wolfowitz, and Chalabi had a personal connection: in 1969, they were introduced and mentored by Albert Wohlstetter, a political science scholar at the University of Chicago, where Wolfowitz and Chalabi were pursuing postgraduate degrees. Furthermore, Perle had dated Wohlstetter's daughter. Wohlstetter also connected Zalmay Khalizad, former United States ambassador to Afghanistan, Iraq, and United Nations, with this group, as Khalizad received his Ph.D. from the University of Chicago.

***

I first began looking into the Iraqi opposition when I read a memo from Peter Rodman saying that we were going to start training opposition forces for the invasion, and I noticed how much this was going to cost.[14] The Iraq Liberation Act (ILA), passed by Congress and signed by President Clinton in 1998, not only called for Saddam's removal, but also for financial assistance to groups that opposed him to the tune of $97 million. The Bush administration cited the ILA to support their invasion of Iraq, as it was an existing policy that they had inherited. What I found so shocking about Rodman's memo

---

14 ██████████████████████████████████████
██████████████████████████████████████
████████████████████████

was that we had just started our campaign in Afghanistan, yet were already planning to invade Iraq. Such an act would take away important resources from Afghanistan, including the funds needed for intelligence analysts to track down Al-Qaeda and Bin Laden, the true culprits of 9/11.[15]

Rodman wanted to start the training, assistance, and advice to the Iraq Opposition quickly. The plan was to get them vetted and into Iraq quickly. The Defense Intelligence Agency (DIA) complained mercifully that they did not have the resources, but their complaining fell to deaf ears. All the Iraqi planning negatively impacted the efforts of fighting the true 9/11 terrorists in Afghanistan. It took over 40 analysts and that was not enough to get the job done at the pace Rodman wanted. DIA had to ask for help from other agencies.

As far as the neocons were concerned, there was no stopping this war. Saddam's fatal error was miscalculating the seriousness of the Bush administration's agenda. Saddam helped perpetrate the ruse of having WMDs. He wanted to keep Iran wary of Iraq following the Iran-Iraq War of 1980. The intelligence community briefed the Pentagon on this. Saddam didn't think the United States would actually invade his country, which aligned precisely with the hopes of the

---

15 ██████████████████████████████████████
██████████████████████████████████████
██████████████████████ Other agencies eventually had to take resources away from tracking Bin Laden, Al-Qaeda, and other threats to help vet potential opposition forces. On December 5, 2002, Paul Wolfowitz was asked to send a memo to these agencies to help expedite the vetting. █████████████████████████████
██████████████████████████████████████
██████████████████████████████████████

Bush administration. They needed time to get our troops in place and surprise Saddam.

***

When Saddam finally realized that the Americans weren't bluffing, he reached out to try and prevent the attack. On March 5, 2003, Imad Hage, a Lebanese American business-man with ties to some of Saddam Hussein's closest advisors, made an overture to the United States.The Pentagon knew that Hage's olive branch was credible, because Richard Perle, one of Donald Rumsfeld's security advisors, had already met with him in London. However, the Pentagon refused to enter-tain Hage. A memo dated March 6, 2003, from Doug Feith to Rumsfeld recommended that the Department of Defense and the Bush administration not respond to Hage. They felt that if it was widely known that the United States was consider-ing Iraq's proposal, it would seem as though Saddam had the upper hand. They were also worried that if France, Germany, and other anti-war UN security council members found out that Saddam was willing to negotiate for peace, they would try to stop any attack. If Hage decided to go public, they made plans to discredit him. Hage was a US citizen with diplomatic status from Liberia and a business located in Lebanon. He had recently been stopped at Dulles Airport for trying to get a gun and a couple of stun guns through security. However, he'd been released because of his diplomatic status. Although Hage was credible, there were also ways he could be discredited.[16]

---

16 ████████████████████████████████████

Once Saddam was certain that the United States was poised to strike, he had given his advisors, including Deputy Prime Minister Tariq Aziz, this blessing to reach out to us. Saddam was willing to give us everything we wanted to prevent war: open elections monitored by the UN; disarmament inspections led by US personnel; support in the global war on terror; first priority in mining rights and oil; and, finally, help in finding solutions to end the Palestinian/Israeli conflict. And yet, the neocons completely rejected Saddam's offer—nothing was going to stop the war.

And off to war we went.

CHAPTER 6

Donald Rumsfeld and His Middle East Doctrine

"There's no debate in the world as to whether they have those weapons. We all know that. A trained ape knows that."

—Donald Rumsfeld, September 2002

I first met Donald Rumsfeld through Richard Myers, and subsequently ran into Rumsfeld a number of times during official military and social events in Washington, D.C. Rumsfeld was always cordial, and I reciprocated his congeniality. However, I was no fan of him. Countless lives were shattered when Rumsfeld ordered our troops to carry out his hegemonic agenda in Iraq. This convinced me that he really didn't care about our troops other than as "boots on the ground."

***

In January 2001, Rumsfeld arrived at the Pentagon for his second tour of duty as secretary of defense, dripping with imperious disdain for the generals and admirals. He thought that they had too much power, so he barged in with an "I'll-show-you-who's-in-charge" attitude. His first encounter with the generals turned into an argument over the notification process regarding a major bombing mission in Iraq. Rumsfeld was incensed; he couldn't tolerate being outside of the chain of command. In his eyes, the chairman of the Joint Chiefs of Staff was "only" an advisor. So, Rumsfeld threw down the gauntlet. He made it known that he and President Bush alone were the ones responsible for operational decisions.

Rumsfeld also took umbrage with the regional four-star general commanders having the title of commander-in-chief (CINC). So, he changed their title to combatant commanders. Rumsfeld said there was only one commander-in-chief, and that was the president. Shortly after that power play, I attended a meeting with one of these four-star generals, who was upset about the decision. Rumsfeld's attitude disgusted him. They would've accepted his changes, however, had Rumsfeld not been so disrespectful of their positions, their service to the country, and their operational experience.[1]

As I mentioned earlier, Rumsfeld liked putting his thoughts down on paper, including the details of the dressing down he gave general officers. For example, I saw an October 2001 memo Rumsfeld wrote to Richard Myers and Marine General Peter Pace excoriating the Department of Defense for "not doing its job" in fighting the war on terror. He felt that our military leaders were overly concerned about making decisions that could cost military lives.

In January 2002, Rumsfeld put out a paper titled "Major Directional Decisions" where he used the term "boots on the ground" to describe our service members. Rumsfeld wanted to convey that the United States was willing to take casualties. Thousands of men and women died in these conflicts, yet Rumsfeld couldn't be bothered to take the time to sign condolence letters to the family members who had lost loved ones. Instead, his staff used a signing machine. This imitation signature was no way to honor our fallen heroes. Rumsfeld eventually agreed to sign these letters himself, after the previous practice was disclosed to the public, earning backlash.

---

1   Rumsfeld signed a memo on October 24, 2002, to all senior Department of Defense leaders stating that there is only one Commander-in-Chief in America, and that is the president. He also stated the acronym *CINC* as a title for military officers would be forbidden ("Commander-In-Chief," October 24, 2002).

***

In June 2015, Rumsfeld came under fire after he told the *Times of London* that he felt it was unrealistic for President Bush to pursue democracy in Iraq. Although spreading democracy might have been one of Bush's reasons for going to war, it wasn't one of Rumsfeld's concerns: he merely wanted control. In a note addressed to Doug Feith, Rumsfeld said that he was annoyed that we were unable to resolve Arab/Israeli hostilities. Rumsfeld remembered a call he received from Alf Landon when he served as White House chief of staff under President Gerald Ford. Landon, the Republican governor of Kansas from 1933–1937 and the 1936 Republican presidential nominee, had asked Rumsfeld to tell Ford that Ronald Reagan was "beating him up" on the Panama Canal issue and putting him in a bind. Landon was referring to the 1976 Panama Canal negotiations. During the Republican presidential primary race, Ronald Reagan, then governor of California, said the Panama Canal was ours and we were going to keep it, putting the Ford campaign in a bind. In one of his "snowflake" flurries of letters, Rumsfeld told Paul Wolfowitz and Doug Feith that we've been in a "hair knot" in the Middle East for the last fifty years, with no resolution in sight. Landon reminded him of what Roosevelt used to say: "Create a diversion when in a bind." He also recalled something President Eisenhower had said: "If you can't solve a problem, then enlarge it."[2]

---

2   Another paper that laid out Rumsfeld's thinking was titled "Major Directional Decisions" (I think one dated January 19, 2002, and one dated January 31 2002): 1. Never go backwards. We will lean forward. 2. Can't defeat terrorism in every corner of the world, so attack where we

Those two statements laid the foundation for Donald Rumsfeld's Middle East Doctrine: *Create a diversion* by declaring war on terrorism, starting with Afghanistan. Then, *enlarge the problem* by pursuing the so-called sponsors of terrorism: Iraq (WMD), Syria (chemical weapons), and Iran (nuclear weapons program). Rumsfeld also believed we needed to go on the offensive. In another memo, he again referenced the Alf Landon call. He felt we needed to stop Iraq, Iran, and Syria from sponsoring Hamas and Hezbollah. Rumsfeld was frustrated that the United States was getting blamed by moderate Arab nations such as Egypt and Jordan for the problems in the Middle East. He was furious at those governments because we were "holding them up" while they let us take the hit for the "peace mess."[3]

Although Rumsfeld and Peter Rodman felt that Iraq, Iran, and Syria were responsible for the radicalization spreading across the Middle East, Rumsfeld, surprisingly, never blamed Saudi Arabia, which has always been the chief culprit in spreading radicalization. In fact, he said that Palestinian terrorism was the core issue preventing peace. Rumsfeld felt that we shouldn't negotiate with the so-called terrorists. Instead, we needed to go after them, which would give us the credi-

---

think they are. 3. The United States will not rule out anything. We will not just use cruise missiles. We will use "boots on the ground" anytime and anywhere [Show the United States is willing to take casualties]. 4. No matter what, the United States will remain engaged in the world. Even when attacked, we will continue to exercise world leadership [PNAC ideology]. 5. When the United States is seen as faint hearted or risk averse, the deterrent is weakened.

3   Memo: "Middle East," August 3, 2002.

bility in the Middle East that he was so desperately sure we didn't have. Here we were, the most powerful country in the world, and yet, in Donald Rumsfeld's mind, we were afraid to assert our dominance. "We look impotent in the eyes of the world in our handling of the Middle East," Rumsfeld noted in a talking paper. Furthermore, Rumsfeld said it was time for the president to use the bully pulpit and start going after the "sponsors of terrorists," beginning with Saddam Hussein.

9/11 gave Rumsfeld the perfect opportunity to execute his doctrine of "creating a diversion and enlarging a problem." After 9/11, terrorism would no longer be treated as a law enforcement issue, as had been done by previous administrations, but as a war matter. Invading Iraq would be the first plan of attack in the "War on Terror."[4]

***

I was relieved when it was announced on November 8, 2006, that Rumsfeld had resigned and was being replaced by Robert Gates, following Republican congressional midterm losses attributed to public disdain over the Iraq War. This wasn't surprising, considering the huge disservice Rumsfeld

---

4   In *War and Decision*, page 283, Doug Feith wrote: "Defense Department officials saw the Saddam Hussein problem as an element of the US war on terrorism—as the Joint Staff made clear in its June 2002 Political-Military Strategic Plan for Iraq. That plan referred back to the October 3, 2001, Strategic Guidance for the Defense Department that Abizaid and I had drafted, which framed the war on terrorism as a confrontation with state [Iraq, Iran, and Syria] and nonstate supporters of terrorist groups as well as the terrorist groups [Hamas and Hezbollah] themselves."

CHAPTER 7

Doug Feith: The Architect

"If I have been inaccurate or unfair, I know that people in the government (including members of Congress, who have access to many of the relevant documents) will quickly call me on it."

—Douglas Feith, *War and Decision*

It's never too late to correct history, especially the lying that was used to justify the Iraq War. For twenty years, I waited to call Doug Feith out on his self-serving interpretation of the cherry-picked documents he used to write his book, *War and Decision*. As someone who has reviewed most of the documents that Feith described as having quoted "with attention to accuracy and context," I hereby, after two decades, challenge his interpretation of them. As with Rumsfeld's snowflakes, I spent a lot of time reading and studying Feith's writings. After all, I was part of the team that examined the very documents he referenced in his memoir.

***

Shortly after I started working for the DRT, I learned that Doug Feith was not well-liked in the Pentagon. Some said he was a crook who couldn't be trusted. Gen. Tommy Franks called him "the fucking stupidest person on the planet." Larry Wilkerson agreed. Jay Gardner labeled him "a dangerous man." One of Rumsfeld's closest advisors, Stephen Herbits, referenced him as "a lunatic and evil spawn."

I didn't know too much about the man. As the undersecretary of defense for Policy, he was simply our boss. Eventually, I did a lot of research into both his personal and professional life. In time, I also became acquainted with Feith and his inner circle from my time working in the DRT and I got a chance to form my own opinion from his visits to our hidden office. I would personally say that Doug Feith is a smart, cunning man—a master in the art of deception.

***

Before forming opinions of people, I always try to figure out what makes them tick. An individual's life experience is foundational to their worldview. While researching Feith, I learned about his family's tragic connection to the Holocaust, and how that has guided his hawkish views on the Middle East. Feith's father, Dalck Feith, was held captive and tortured by the Nazis. His grandparents, aunts, and uncles were all killed during the Holocaust. This tragic history, as well as his introduction to the Jewish Institute for National Security Affairs (JINSA) may have shaped Feith's ideology. In fact, JINSA believe that Hamas, Hezbollah, and the countries that support them are in the same league as Nazi Germany. They are certain that these countries are planning to annihilate the Jews in a second Holocaust.

***

Feith was part of Donald Rumsfeld's inner circle. And Feith controlled all of the Pentagon's national security policy and strategy. He had great influence over Rumsfeld, who trusted Feith, due to his stellar writing skills and his ability to stay ahead of him.[1] Feith would draft highly persuasive memos

---

1   In a memo dated July 25, 2006, Rumsfeld defended Feith, saying "Doug Feith is a very bright, talented, dedicated public servant, who did a terrific job for the country."

for Rumsfeld to sign, pushing the case to go to war with cover notes urging Rumsfeld to pass these memos on to the president, to Condoleezza Rice, and to Colin Powell. I never saw Rumsfeld question Feith in any of the snowflakes I read. President Bush was also impressed by Feith's papers, something that Feith often boasted about. In a deliberate move to undermine Powell and the State Department, Feith would on occasion leave out the State Department from the coordination process before sending Department of Defense papers to the president. This was deliberately provocative: on foreign policy issues, the State and Defense departments are supposed to work in coordination. Feith wanted to bypass Powell because he and his inner circle were in a rush to go to war and Powell had deep concerns about that.

I had numerous brief conversations with Feith at the Pentagon. To my surprise, despite his blustery reputation, he came across as demure during our interactions, low-key and even somewhat timid. When his father passed away, I gave him my condolences, which he accepted with humble appreciation. Though our interactions were cordial, I will be forever critical of his foreign policy ideology and the damage he has done to our country. Doug Feith's role in making the case for war in Iraq hurt our national security and almost bankrupted us.

***

When I joined the DRT, I was told our mission was to locate and declassify as many Iraq War documents as possible in anticipation of public demand, due to their historical significance. However, it was rumored that our team was actually assembled to make these documents available to Doug Feith; specifically, for the memoir he was planning to write. This turned out to be true. The DRT's number-one client, after his resignation from the Pentagon, was Doug Feith.

Feith used our services to retrieve and/or declassify memos and documents for his personal use. In fact, the papers he references in *War and Decision* appear with the "declassified by the DRT" stamp, which was the result of our work. The week before Feith's book was released, Ryan Henry, principal deputy to the undersecretary of defense for policy, asked for a report within thirty days, with a recommendation as to whether our declassification project should continue. For me, the timing of Henry's memo was proof enough that the DRT was created to supply Feith with the documents he needed. Furthermore, Feith used our team to cherry-pick which documents he wanted declassified in order to manipulate the narrative in his favor. His book is nothing more than a continuation of the (dis)information strategy of the neocons.

An especially troubling fact is that some of the documents Feith used in his book and that are listed on his website weren't, as far as I know, officially declassified at the time he shared them. When I questioned one senior Department of Defense official about this, he shook his head and told me, "We know, but what can we do about it? It's already out there now." Even worse, before the book's release, there was even some talk among senior advisors in the Office of the Secretary of Defense (OSD) that Feith probably wouldn't hold off publication, even if a full security review hadn't been completed yet. Feith was paranoid about anyone seeing the book, for fear of it being leaked. He felt that people were out to get him.[2]

If he were still alive, Carl Levin—the former Democratic senator from Michigan—would agree about our team's true purpose as only existing to help Feith. In the introduction to his memoir, Feith claimed that members of Congress had equal access to the documents he quoted. This was a lie. Donald Rumsfeld ignored most of Levin's requests for documents. Levin was deemed "not privileged enough" to access them, despite the fact that, at the time, Carl Levin was *the* ranking member of the Senate Armed Services Committee. The truth is, the Pentagon hawks simply didn't trust Levin.[3]

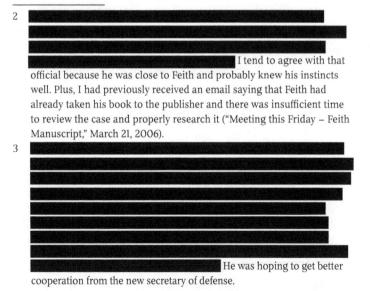

2 ███████████████████████████████████████
███████████████████████████████████████
███████████████████████████ I tend to agree with that
official because he was close to Feith and probably knew his instincts
well. Plus, I had previously received an email saying that Feith had
already taken his book to the publisher and there was insufficient time
to review the case and properly research it ("Meeting this Friday – Feith
Manuscript," March 21, 2006).

3 ███████████████████████████████████████
███████████████████████████████████████
███████████████████████████████████████
███████████████████████████████████████
███████████████████████████████████████
███████████████████████████████████████
███████████████████████████████████████
███████████████████████████████████████
██████████████████████████ He was hoping to get better
cooperation from the new secretary of defense.

The DRT team also had a few visits from the Special Inspector General for Iraq Reconstruction (SIGIR). SIGIR was established in 2004 and led by Stuart Bowen, who was responsible for auditing and investigating the money obligated for the Iraq reconstruction and operations effort. He wanted to review our Pentagon internal documents to see if there was any information in our library that could aid his team's efforts. Early on, SIGIR encountered difficulty getting the documents, as there were folks in OSD Policy who were reluctant to support SIGIR's request. However, after some hard work and determination, SIGIR was able to secure some of our declassified documents.

During his investigation, Bowen discovered various instances of reconstruction frauds, waste, and abuse. Bowen presented his final report to Congress in March of 2013. The report revealed that approximately $8 billion had been lost to fraud, wasted, or outright stolen, by both Americans and Iraqis. For example, one American service member received millions of dollars in kickbacks, while some Iraqi officials used American dollars to purchase second-rate military equipment. I am proud that the DRT played such a role in the development of this report.

***

I place a lot of the war's blame squarely on Doug Feith's shoulders. Most of the deceit was devised by him and his immediate—and secretive—inner circle: Peter Rodman, Abe Shulsky, William Luti, and Paul Wolfowitz, who was probably the biggest war hawk at the Pentagon. This circle ran a special intelligence unit that undermined the Defense Intelligence Agency (DIA), the CIA, and the State Department's efforts to find links between Iraq and Al-Qaeda, and to confirm that Iraq had WMD. There was always a question as to whether the Pentagon created this special unit or if it was a covert, unauthorized operation. Regardless, this unit definitely existed, Feith was behind it, and Rumsfeld allowed it to conduct its business. It seems to me as though they were breaking the law, since Congress funds the CIA to do that sort of intelligence business, not the Department of Defense.

When it came to finding links between Al-Qaeda and Saddam, the OSD discounted most of the DIA's and CIA's intelligence work. Feith distrusted both agencies since he felt that they weren't loyal enough to his cause. Feith and Wolfowitz only wanted intelligence that supported the case of the neocons, but the DIA and CIA were not giving them what they wanted. So Feith, Wolfowitz, and their ilk accused these two agencies of incompetence.

Ironically, I've seen a number of interviews where Doug Feith blamed the CIA for supplying the wrong intelligence regarding WMD. However, ███████████████████████ ██████████████████████████████████ no smoking gun. The CIA didn't know if WMD actually existed, and, if they did exist, they had no idea where they were hidden. However, Paul Wolfowitz was hell-bent on proving otherwise, so his team turned to other sources, such as Ahmed Chalabi and INC, who supplied Wolfowitz with the intel he wanted, whether true or not. One of these sources, Rafid Ahmed Alwan al-Janabi—code name "Curveball"—defected to Germany from Iraq in 1999. He became an intelligence source in Germany, saying that Saddam had WMD. However, he was lying. Although Germany discounted Curveball when the truth emerged, the United States had no qualms about using his fabrications as justification to go to war.

How had Doug Feith even been confirmed for such a senior Pentagon position with his shady background? After all, in 1992, when Feith was on the National Security Council, it was alleged that he had given secrets to the Israeli embassy. Feith has strong ties to the pro-Israel lobby, as well as to Israel's right-wing Likud Party, which doesn't support a Palestinian state. In fact, I saw a note that Feith wrote where he proudly said that he was a good friend of Benjamin Netanyahu, and had made personal phone calls to him during the buildup to the Iraq War. Feith was the designated coordinator and point man to Israel. It concerns me when such a high-ranking individual in the American government is that close to the inner workings of another country, working as possible lobbyist for this country without disclosing his double allegiance. Condoleezza Rice even chastised Feith on several occasions for "carrying the mail" for Netanyahu's Likud Party.

Feith was eventually forced to resign. On August 8, 2005, I attended his farewell gathering at the Pentagon auditorium. I almost fell out of my seat when Peter Pace, vice chairman of the Joint Chiefs of Staff, said, "It irritates me that anyone would question [Feith's] loyalty or his motives. He cares only about what is best for the United States." Though I respect Pace and think he's a great person, I completely disagree with him. Feith's actions are more than enough to create suspicion about his true motivations.

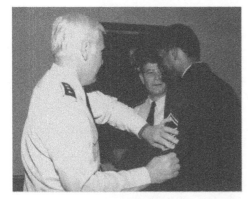

Lieutenant General Buster Glosson (architect of the air campaign for Operation Desert Storm) congratulating Fritz on his promotion to the highest enlisted rank.

Then-Colonel Ed Eberhart chatting with Fritz. Eberhart went on to become a four-star general and commander of NORAD, and was in command on 9/11.

Chief Fritz (second from left) on a visit to Korea to observe military drills and operations.

Chief Fritz on an Air Force One flight with President George W. Bush and First Lady Laura Bush.

Chief Fritz

Fritz (at far right) on stage with Secretary of Defense Donald Rumsfeld, Senator Bob Dole, Chairman of the Joint Chiefs General Hugh Shelton, and the other joint chiefs.

General Myers awarding Fritz the Legion of Merit for his outstanding leadership and performance at Air Force Space Command.

Command Chief Fritz bids farewell to President Bill Clinton as Fritz's wife Debra and former Secretary of State Madeleine Albright look on.

CHAPTER 8

**General Richard Myers:
A Man of Conviction**

I've had the pleasure of knowing General Richard Myers for thirty years. Myers was the top wartime general and a key figure during the invasions of Afghanistan and Iraq. I was his senior enlisted advisor during his major command assignments, and I consider him to be the best boss a person could have. He remains a good friend to this day. Although I disagreed with him about our invasion of Iraq, I will always stand by him. Even during the stress of managing two wars, Myers carved out time to preside over my retirement ceremony from the military, an honor I'll never forget. He also bestowed upon me one of the highest non-battle performance decorations an enlisted person can receive: the Legion of Merit.

At first, Myers thought he was going to retire after the NORAD/Space Command job, and surely thought he was done after his tenure as vice chairman of the Joint Chiefs of Staff was over. Although it may have crossed his mind, he never thought he would instead receive the most senior military position in the Department of Defense. However, as an already trusted advisor to the secretary of defense, Richard Myers became the fifteenth chairman of the Joint Chiefs of Staff in October 2001, serving as the principal military advisor to President Bush, Donald Rumsfeld, and the National Security Council for the next four years.

***

In *State of Denial,* his book about the Iraq War, Bob Woodward criticizes our military leaders, in particular Myers and Peter Pace, who was the Vice Chairman, categorizing them as weak. He thought we needed someone like George Patton or Douglas MacArthur to handle Donald Rumsfeld. In Woodward's view, the Joint Chiefs of Staff were nothing more than "yes men." I disagree. Rather, Myers is someone who respects the civilian authority of the military but who refuses to publicly contradict his bosses. That's Myers's philosophy and his conviction. However, I will say that I always wanted him to be tougher with Rumsfeld during their Pentagon press conferences. I hope that he at least called out Rumsfeld behind closed doors. During our periodic conversations after my retirement, Myers assured me that he didn't hold back any of his concerns in private.

***

On March 17, 2003, three days before American bombs and missiles started dropping on Iraq, I sent Myers a frank email. I confided to him that, among the troops, there was a lot of confusion and anxiety about the mission. They were questioning the motives, as most didn't see Iraq as a credible threat. I wanted Myers to reassure me that we were doing the right thing. But I didn't get the assurance I was hoping for. Like Powell, Myers was a career military officer who believed that the duty of the troops was to give excellent advice and then to carry out the Commander-in-Chief's orders, even if we disagreed. I couldn't do that.

Many people would ask me why Myers didn't resign in protest, considering how badly Rumsfeld ran things. Because I didn't want to inquire directly, I asked some of the senior officers who worked with Myers about that. They said Myers was frustrated with Rumsfeld. They said that he wanted to quit and that he almost did. But ultimately, he couldn't bring himself to throw in the towel. Myers believed he had to hang tough, despite his feelings about Donald Rumsfeld. As much as I respect Myers for his decision to stay the course, I must confess there were many times I wished he would've slapped Rumsfeld and told him to "take this job and shove it." When I shared this with Myers, he laughed, but wanted to make sure I understood that he did not feel that way. As he told me during one of our breakfast meetings, he never hesitated to give his advice and recommendations. However, he also told me that he believed Iraq had WMD. He fell for Curveball's intel.

When some of the generals came out against Rumsfeld, Myers spoke out against them. I had a conversation with Myers about this. I told Myers that I hoped that the Bush administration wasn't taking advantage of him. I told him that if he believed generals shouldn't speak out against civilian leadership, then we shouldn't let civilian leaders embroil general officers in their political battles, either. Myers assured me that the administration hadn't put him up to it. He wasn't defending Rumsfeld, per se, but simply giving his opinion. To set the record straight, Myers clarified that generals were allowed to debate leadership during the run-up to any war, if the generals disagreed with the issues.

***

In 2006, I tried to get Richard Myers to run for president, as an Independent, which he thought was crazy on my part. Although Myers was tainted by his association with the Iraq War and knew it would be a long shot, he did have name recognition and possessed solid military experience. In addition, he was an outstanding consensus, coalition, and alliance-builder, a sorely needed quality during one of the most polarizing times in history. Equipped with those traits, I thought Myers could mend the nation and restore our standing internationally. I laid out for him what I thought was a great platform, including critical debate about the war. I also suggested that he consider asking Oprah Winfrey to be his running mate, my rationale being that she was smart, world-famous, had a strong female following, and could counter Hillary Clinton, whom I thought would be the Democratic nominee. Not to mention that Winfrey could raise a lot of money. Barack Obama agreed: when the then-senator from Illinois appeared on *The Late Show with David Letterman* to present his Top Ten list, Obama's number-one was "Oprah for Vice President."

Despite all this, Myers wanted nothing to do with running for president. In fact, he loathed politics. Although he appreciated my efforts, he sent me an email saying that "I needed to find another horse to ride." I chuckled at that. I realized that Myers was aware that I was trying to convey my own message, issues, and politics through him, because he had the public recognition I lacked. Still, that got me thinking. I decided to ride my own horse and ran for Congress in 2014 and 2018, albeit unsuccessfully.

In May 2008, I saw Myers at the Pentagon. He said he still liked the platform I laid out for him two years earlier, but reiterated that he wouldn't pull the lever for himself as president when it came time to vote. I kindly said we should've had the opportunity. He smiled, waved to me, said thank you, and departed. As I always did, I told him that he was a good man.

***

I thought our political conversations would end there. But after noticing how hard the neocons were pushing John McCain for president in order to continue their Middle East policy, I decided that I had to do something to prevent that from happening. I started pressuring retired senior officers and other military members, including Myers, to back Barack Obama. I felt it would be dangerous if McCain were to become president, for it was clear that the neocons would surely control his foreign policy. There was no doubt in my mind that the neocons had their eye on Iran and—worst of all—were planning a new Cold War with Russia. After numerous email exchanges and a couple of meetings, I thought that I had convinced Myers that Obama was the right man for the job, even though Myers had concerns about Obama's foreign policy experience. After much debate, I think Myers, like other senior officers, thought Obama was the better choice. The officers felt that McCain was too overbearing and had a know-it-all attitude. In fact, a senior general officer confided in me that he hated McCain and that McCain hated him, so he was looking forward to "poking McCain in the eye" by supporting Obama.

As the race between McCain and Obama tightened, I asked Myers to publicly endorse Obama. Myers refused. He said that although he supported Obama, he also felt that senior officers—whether active or retired—shouldn't be publicly involved in politics. When Colin Powell came out in support of Obama, I urged Myers to do the same. I knew that some Republicans would lash out at Powell, claiming that he endorsed Obama only because they were both Black (and sure enough, Rush Limbaugh and other far-right zealots didn't let me down). So, I again asked Myers to come out for Obama, to lend credibility to Powell's endorsement. After all, if he were to do so, Myers would be yet another former chairman of the Joint Chiefs of Staff voicing support for Obama. The far right would have no response to that. Myers told me he would consider it, but he also admitted that he thought an open endorsement wouldn't make a difference. I pushed back, telling him that many of the retired senior officers who liked and respected Myers would feel more comfortable about supporting Obama publicly if Myers did so himself. Myers still seemed hesitant. I knew I had to do something drastic.

***

I knew Scott Gration from my days as Myers's principal advisor in the Pacific, when he was the commander of one of our bases in Alaska. Now retired, Gration also happened to be one of Obama's top military and foreign policy advisors. He eventually became the United States ambassador to Kenya. Ironically, in 2012 Gration was fired for allegedly using a personal email account to conduct State Department business. This incident was brought up a few years later, during the inquiries into Hillary Clinton's similar use of a personal email account. I decided to call Gration and to ask him what he thought of Myers publicly endorsing Obama. He loved the idea, believing it would be a boon to Obama's presidential bid. I told Gration that I couldn't convince Myers that his endorsement would actually make a difference. So, Gration and I both came up with a plan that we thought would persuade Myers to change his mind.

My initial thought was to have Gration call Myers. However, Gration had a better idea: Have Obama himself call Myers. We decided to set up that call on October 29, 2008, the night Obama was to unveil a half-hour infomercial on all major TV networks, right before he was set to appear on stage with Bill Clinton for the first time. Thus, we had to move fast—we only had a small window of opportunity to connect the two of them together. Gration was to call Obama's campaign staff, and I was to reach out to Myers to give him a heads up. I didn't want him to get blindsided. I reached out to Myers and asked if he would take a call from Senator Obama. At first, Myers thought I was kidding. But when he finally realized I was dead serious, he doubled down on his conviction that senior officers should stay away from politics. Yet when I told Myers how important his endorsement must mean to Obama—so much so that he was willing to make the effort to reach out—this gave him pause. Though he wouldn't promise anything, he said he was willing to talk to Obama. Elated, I told Myers to stand by and that I would get back to him immediately.

Meanwhile, Gration was eagerly awaiting confirmation, as he had already coordinated with Obama's staff. The small window we had secured was closing fast. We had less than thirty minutes to make the call happen. I went back to Myers and told him that Obama's call was about to come through, and I asked him to ring me afterward. The half hour came and went, and I still hadn't heard anything from either Myers or Gration. I was anxious. Finally, my phone rang. It was Gration. And it was exactly what I had dreaded: an apology. Obama was running late to meet Bill Clinton, so they had to delay the call. But there was a silver lining. Gration assured me that Obama would call Myers the next morning, around eleven, but we had to be flexible.

After I hung up with Gration, my biggest concern wasn't the thought of phoning Myers to apologize for the canceled call, but rather having to ask him for more time to think it over. To my relief, Myers wasn't upset. In fact, he was totally fine waiting until the morning.

The following day, at 11:10 a.m., I was sitting in my office when I received an email from Myers, asking me to call him right away on his cell phone. My heart raced. I dialed Myers's number and when he picked up, he informed me that he had just spoken to Obama. Although he appreciated Obama's call, this alone wasn't enough to convince him to go public. And that was the end of it.

Sure, I was disappointed. Yet I couldn't help admiring Myers. Through thick and thin, the man remained true to his convictions. Most importantly, I was impressed at how graciously Obama accepted Myers's refusal. Although Myers wouldn't go public, Obama appreciated his support and would still seek him out for wise counsel in the future.

***

During his presidential campaign, Obama said that he wanted to reach out to every potential voter and shake their hand. Obama's overtures to Myers proved to me that this was true. Although Obama knew that Richard Myers was tied to the Bush administration, he still reached out to him in good faith. That says a lot. As I said before, Richard Myers is the best boss a person could ever have. He is a man of true conviction.

CHAPTER 9

The (Dis)information Strategy

"The Iraq War was sold to the American people with a sophisticated 'political propaganda campaign' and aimed at 'manipulating sources of public opinion' and 'downplaying the major reason for going to war.'"

—Former White House Press Secretary Scott McClellan in *What Happened: Inside the Bush White House and Washington's Culture of Deception*

Abe Shulsky and Doug Feith masterminded a large portion of the Iraq War's propaganda campaign out of the Pentagon's Policy Office. Feith felt that the White House wasn't doing enough to come up with a strategy that legitimized their agenda. After all, if the American people knew the real reasons we went to war, they probably wouldn't have supported the invasion. So, on behalf of the Bush administration, Shulsky and Feith orchestrated a plan to manipulate public opinion.

Their plan, which they called the Information Strategy, aggressively sold the war by flooding the media with disinformation. The key component of their strategy was a public-affairs plan they called the Iraq Surrogates and Influential Outreach Program. Shulsky and Feith courted prominent former Cabinet members, congressional representatives, retired generals, officers, scholars, and members of the press who were willing to make the case for war. These surrogates were provided briefings and talking points by senior administration officials. They held special meetings with Donald Rumsfeld and they were part of an exclusive email list. As long as they remained loyal, they were kept in the loop by the neocons. Henry Kissinger, former Secretary of Defense James Schlesinger, and Ken Adelman, a former diplomat and assistant to Rumsfeld, were three of the top officials who signed on as surrogates. In February and April 2003, Adelman authored two *Washington Post* editorials, "Cakewalk in

Iraq" and "Cakewalk Revisited," where he confidently predicted an easy victory in Iraq (Adelman later admitted that
he may have been wrong about pushing so hard for war).
Kissinger was not only a surrogate, but a key advisor on
strategy as well.

The architects of the disinformation strategy also
recruited members of the press to promote their scheme by
leaking false information. For example, the neocons were in
cahoots with Judith Miller, a former *New York Times* reporter
who wrote several think pieces bolstering the baseless claim
that Saddam had WMD. In 2004, Miller even went to jail
for refusing to reveal her source after leaking the identity
of the CIA officer Valerie Plame in an attempt to discredit
her. Her source happened to be Scooter Libby. The neocons
also solicited retired generals to sell the war to the American
people. Shulsky and Feith had studied polls showing that the
public trusted the US military, so they felt the public would
view these generals more favorably. Those who signed on
to the plan saw the benefits of having access to Rumsfeld. It
gave them an opportunity to remain relevant.

Tom McInerney, a former Air Force assistant vice chief
of staff and a Fox News military analyst, was one such surrogate. He came to the Pentagon as the third top official
for the Air Staff just as I was ending my first Pentagon tour
as part of the Air Force Headquarters Staff. At the time,
I admired McInerney. Earlier in his career, he had been
awarded the Order of the Sword, the highest honor bestowed
upon enlisted personnel in recognition of outstanding leadership. McInerney mastered the neocons' pro-war talking

points. At the September 2002 Senate Armed Services committee hearing on the United States's policy toward Iraq, he stated: "The issue is, does Iraq, as a terrorist state, get weapons of mass destruction in the hands of terrorists, just like he's influenced the PLO [Palestine Liberation Organization]? . . . . we must make some decisions, because you can't react after a nuclear weapon goes off in this country." Neither Bush, Cheney, Rumsfeld, nor Wolfowitz could have said it any better.

McInerney made the case for "anticipatory self-defense," tying Saddam to Al-Qaeda and Bin Laden. He instilled fear by alluding to the possibility of a Saddam-instigated attack that could rival 9/11. Regarding the conflict between Palestine and Israel, McInerney also said, "I don't think that will be solved until Iraq comes down."

In March 2013, I had the opportunity to meet with Tom McInerney and challenge him on his role in spreading disinformation. I introduced him to some of the wounded warriors. Meeting them touched him so deeply that he tried to get me to understand his point of view. McInerney told me that he took the 9/11 attacks personally, and blamed them on those he thinks sponsor terrorism: Iraq, Syria, and Iran. He believed the only way to stop terrorism was through aggressive military engagement with hostile regimes. In order to better comprehend his views, he gave me a copy of his book *Endgame*. I did read it, but it seemed just like more neocon propaganda. During our conversations, McInerney mentioned the need to take on Saudi Arabia as well. I agreed with him on that, as Saudi factions do fund terrorism. Yet, we didn't hear much about the Saudis from the Bush administration following 9/11.

I was also extremely disappointed with Tom McInerney for giving credence to the "Birther" movement. In August 2010, he supplied an affidavit in support of Army Lieutenant Colonel Terrence Lakin, who was facing trial for refusing to obey orders from President Obama because of his belief that the commander-in-chief wasn't a natural-born American citizen.[1] In my view, that is as close to what we in the military call "subversion" as it gets. Not surprisingly, I later found out that McInerney, like Gen. Mike Flynn, supported Donald Trump's election lie, even going as far as recommending that Trump declare martial law. I now understand what Richard Myers meant when he told me that generals, active or retired, should stay out of politics.

***

The Information Strategy even carried over into the war itself. The neocons' biggest coup was the spread of Al-Qaeda in Iraq. When it was perceived that we were failing at "winning the hearts and minds of the Iraqis," ███████████

████████████████████████████████████

████████████████████████████████████

---

1   In his affidavit, McInerney stated: "It is my opinion that LTC Lakin's request for discovery relating to the president's birth records in Hawaii is absolutely essential to determining not merely his guilt or innocence but to reassuring all military personnel once and for all for this president whether his service as Commander-in-Chief is Constitutionally proper." McInerney's affidavit could have put doubt in the minds of many officers he may have mentored in the past.

The neocons felt they could sway public opinion if they convinced the American people that we had to stay the course in Iraq to fight Al-Qaeda, even though we knew the Shiites would never allow Al-Qaeda to dominate their country. Al-Qaeda is led by Sunnis. So, the Bush administration used Al-Qaeda as an offensive weapon in their disinformation campaign. They wanted the public to believe that we had to fight Al-Qaeda in Iraq in retaliation for 9/11—even though 9/11 was orchestrated in Afghanistan. Many of our citizens were duped into thinking that we invaded Iraq to prevent Al-Qaeda from becoming a domestic problem. Some folks even believed we would literally have to fight Arab terrorists on our streets. Even as late as 2015, Lindsay Graham was advocating that we needed to invade Syria to prevent the Islamic State from taking over America.

---

2   Memo: "Our Iraq propaganda efforts must change Gears," September 1, 2003.

CHAPTER 10

Why Bush Had to Stay the Course

"Leaving Iraq will be decided by a later president."
—George W. Bush, in response to a press question
on Iraq withdrawal plans, March 21, 2006

As long as he was president, George W. Bush could not leave Iraq in shambles under the control of a Shia-dominated regime. The Sunni countries would then descend on Iraq, igniting a civil war that would spread like wildfire throughout the region. Bush's policies, and the United States, would have been blamed for that.

Bush's biggest concern about leaving Iraq was displeasing Saudi Arabia. The Saudis play a significant role in the world economy and their support is critical for countering terrorism, as well as helping negotiate any future Arab-Israeli peace deals. The Saudis had their own reason for wanting Saddam out of Iraq. Saudi Arabia was battling Iraq over Sunni dominion in the Middle East, and Saddam had threatened Saudi Arabia on numerous occasions. The Saudis didn't view Israel as a threat to their security: their issues with Israel were based on the Palestinian plight. Ultimately, Saudi Arabia was willing to support the Iraq invasion if it eliminated Saddam, their biggest menace.[1]

The Saudis felt they had the most to lose if a weakened and hostile Saddam remained in power. Although Saddam was also a Sunni, he wanted to be the foremost Arab leader in the region. The Saudis knew that many in the Arab world

---

1   Crown Prince Abdullah of Saudi Arabia told Kurdish leader Farr Barzani in November 2001 that the Americans were not serious about truly taking out Saddam. Abdullah said, "If they are serious, we would support." Rodman to SecDef memo, "Saudi Views of Iraq," November 27, 2001.

admired Saddam for his willingness to stand up to the United States. They were also aware that many believed the Saudi Kingdom was merely a US puppet. Along with Israel and the United Kingdom, Saudi Arabia was the only other country we kept informed about our plans to invade Iraq.

At first, the Saudis were worried the Americans would destabilize Iraq and then leave. The Bush administration reassured them that this wouldn't be the case. After all, Bush's legacy was on the line. He promised that we wouldn't leave until the job was done. He promised not to repeat the same mistakes that we made getting out of Vietnam, Somalia, Lebanon, and Iraq in the first Gulf War. He promised that we wouldn't abandon Iraq until it was safe, secure, and friendly to Saudi Arabia.

The Saudis tried to hold Bush to his promise. However, although we got rid of Saddam, we failed at everything else. Iraq became a mess. In the fall of 2006, King Abdullah, the Saudi monarch, summoned Dick Cheney to discuss his concerns. Abdullah told Cheney that Saudi Arabia would offer financial backing to the Sunnis in Iraq if we were to pull out of the region altogether. Even though Bush had kept his original promise, the Saudis were displeased with the growing ties between Nouri al-Maliki—Iraq's new, US-appointed post-war prime minister—and Iran, an alliance which was leaving Saudi Arabia vulnerable. The Saudis eventually did end up providing financial aid to Sunni factions in Iraq.

Bush knew that if Iran tried to take over Iraq, the Saudis would counter this attempt. Bush had reasons for concern: After all, Saudi Arabia always had the option to let loose their powerful terrorist network. In 2006, Great Britain was told by the Saudis to cease a bribery investigation implicating their Prince Bandar in 2006. If Great Britain refused, Saudi

Arabia warned that it would cut off their cooperation on counterterrorism operations. In response, the British government halted the investigation, citing "national security concerns." Forty-five percent of all foreign militants targeting US troops and Iraqi Shiites were Saudi Arabians. Most of the 9/11 hijackers were Saudi.

Moreover, the Saudis could disrupt the world's oil supply. Why do you think we never officially condemned Saudi Arabia for its role in 9/11, even though Saudis carried out more suicide bombings than any other foreign fighters and provided money to Al-Qaeda? The Bush administration put Iraq, Syria, and Iran on its hit list, but never Saudi Arabia. Bush knew that the Saudis could become the United States's worst nightmare if we crossed them. If Saudi Arabia were to cut off its oil supply from the global economy, the world's banking system would collapse.

***

Bush kept his word, leaving it up to his successor to deal with Iraq. It took a lot of guts for President Obama to keep his campaign promise of getting us out of Iraq, a decision which caused more chaos. The neocons argued that if we had instead negotiated a status-of-forces agreement and hadn't pulled out, Iraq would have become a peaceful, democratized ally. They now contend that Iraq is separated along sectarian lines and is therefore ground zero for the region's battle for supremacy between Shiite Iran and Sunni Saudi Arabia. There is no question that we must now also deal with the remnants of the Islamic State, which some believe the Saudis fund. No matter who is ultimately to blame, we have turned Iraq—and the entire region—into a ticking time bomb.

CHAPTER 11

The Insurgency, and How
Iraq Became a Mess

Ike Skelton's concerns were justified: the reconstruction process was a total disaster. Iraq did indeed become a "damn mess," ending up on the verge of civil war. The Shiites dominated the country, giving Iran influence in Iraq. Saddam had acted as a buffer between Iran and the rest of the region,

---

1   Briefing for Representative Skelton, September 18, 2002.

preventing Iran from overtaking the Persian Gulf. Getting rid of Saddam emboldened Iran's aggression.

The inability to rebuild Iraq was an abject failure on our part. Furthermore, Rumsfeld and Paul Wolfowitz also discounted the expert advice of General Eric Shinseki, the Chief of Staff of the Army at the time. They claimed Shinseki was off the mark when he said we needed to send 300,000 troops to successfully fend off an insurgency and maintain peace between the internal factions—the Sunnis, Shias, and the Turks in the north. Shinseki and Colin Powell understood that once combat operations ceased, we needed serious reinforcements. Rumsfeld said that he took to heart the commanders' advice on how to keep Iraq stable. But we didn't have enough troops—the maximum sent over was 15,000—because both Rumsfeld and Dick Cheney felt we had deployed more than enough soldiers during the first Gulf War. Rumsfeld and Cheney even disregarded the CIA's warnings about an insurgency in Iraq. General Tommy Franks, the commander of Central Command (CENTCOM), said his three highest priorities in Iraq were to defeat its military, find WMDs, and protect the oil fields.

In his book, Doug Feith gave a veiled

answer as to why we didn't have enough troops: "I think Rumsfeld influenced Franks's thinking on the issue of force levels. Especially in early stages of working on the Iraq war plan, Rumsfeld reminded Franks of the large excess of men and equipment that had been sent to the theater for Desert Storm in 1990–91."

There was a reconstruction plan, but we couldn't implement it due to the insurgency. Besides, keeping the peace was of lesser concern to the neocons, compared to protecting the oil fields and refineries. I read an internal memo from the Office of the Secretary of Defense (OSD) stating that the plan lacked cohesion and cooperation. On February 3, 2003, Col. Steve Busby prepared a memo and point paper, signed by Assistant Secretary of Defense Chris Lamb, for Doug Feith. Busby warned Feith about the dangers of not "keeping the peace" in Iraq. Lamb admitted that our efforts could fail, due to the lack of detailed planning and the limited number of forces sent to Iraq. █████████████████████████

██

██

██

The Office of Reconstruction and Humanitarian Assistance (ORHA), headed by Army Lt. Gen. Jay Gardner, was established with the help of the international community to ease the transition to a new Iraqi-led government. However,

---

██

███████████████████████████

3   Briefing—"Civil Administration," February 20, 2003.

the ORHA didn't receive the resources it thought it would get from CENTCOM. Gardner was under the impression that CENTCOM would provide military police to keep the peace. But CENTCOM had other priority missions in the Middle East, Afghanistan, and Africa, and thus they weren't able to send enough troops to Iraq.

Doug Feith said Tommy Franks wanted no part of civil unrest duties in Iraq, and he was right. Franks left that up to Jay Gardner, who, as mentioned above, wasn't handed enough resources to carry out the task. On April 16, 2003, Franks sent a message to Donald Rumsfeld, saying that major military operations were over: "Iraqi people are free of Regime and oil fields are safe. Start next phase (I think IV) of Reconstruction." (Translation: "I'm out of here.")

We wanted to gain the Iraqi people's support by quickly restarting industry, by boosting employment, and by implementing humanitarian programs. We wanted to restore electricity, banking, water, and sewage. We wanted to protect oil resources. However, there was one problem: the insurgency led by former Baath Party military members, Islamic fundamentalists, and Shiite forces. Someone at the top failed to follow up on the plan to quell civil unrest. After all, Tommy Franks was only concerned with his three primary goals (combat operations, WMD, and protecting the oil fields). Everything else was up in the air. I read an email where Steve Busby told CENTCOM that the guidance regarding Iraq was "Do what you can with what you have."

***

Our reconstruction effort was known as the Three-tier Public Order Plan. Tier One was to contain public disorder to minimize the impact on combat operations. We assumed that we would have up to 50,000 police officers at our disposal to do that, even though we had disbanded the Iraqi police soon after ousting Saddam. Tier Two would create a Quick Reaction Force to respond to an immediate crisis. In Tier Three, if the disturbance jeopardized keeping the peace, we would call on reserve forces or units to finish the assigned combat tasks.[4] The entire plan fell apart on the first day. Chaos ensued in Iraq immediately, dashing any attempt at reconstruction.

Chris Lamb warned that Shiite forces would attack what remained of Saddam's Baath Party. However, Rumsfeld and Cheney maintained their stubborn belief that our military victory would curtail any insurgency. The neocons went to war with a plan for quick success but without a clear vision of how to keep the peace afterward.

After some members of the press, military experts, and other political pundits accused the Pentagon of not adequately preparing for the postwar period, folks on the inside began questioning what went wrong, trying to figure out who was at fault. In his book, Doug Feith blamed Tommy Franks. On September 11, 2003, Lamb sent Feith a memo stating that he, Lamb, provided a postwar plan to avert civil disorder. Yet the memo was never addressed by the time it got to the secretary of defense's office. In addition, major

---

4   Summary of Public Order Plan, undated.

infighting played out in the public over who had disbanded the Iraqi army. Some officials felt that this decision added fuel to the insurgency.

Interestingly, Rumsfeld later said that he didn't recall who disbanded the army. On October 28, 2004, he sent Feith a snowflake asking who was responsible for this, Jay Gardner or Paul Bremer? Bremer had been the leader of the Coalition Provisional Authority, which oversaw the implementation of a transitional government in Iraq. That snowflake snowballed into a massive blame game, resulting in no conclusive answer. Robert Draper's book *Dead Certain: The Presidency of George W. Bush* also raised the question of who gave the order. Bush claimed that he had been against disbanding the Iraqi army and was surprised by the decision. But Bremer sent memos to *The New York Times* supporting his claim that the president knew exactly what was going on. Bremer denied that this decision was his doing, saying that the army had dissolved on its own.

This was a boldfaced lie.

███

███
███
████████████████████████████████████ Three days after sending that memo, Bremer placed the official order disbanding the army. He also fired many of Iraq's mid-level state officials—a major mistake. These individuals could

---

5 ██
  ██████████████████████████████████

have kept some form of functioning government in place. Furthermore, Bremer refused to give many of these officials their back pay and pensions. This callous disregard led to general dissatisfaction with all Americans, paving the way for the rise of the Islamic State.

CHAPTER 12

What We Fight (Religious War)

According to a memo to Doug Feith ██████████████
██
██
██
██[1]

Andrews's concern was that the continuous use of the term "War on Terror" put us in a no-win box. You can't defeat a movement, he explained. There are no official armies or navies in an ideological battle. In addition, the opposition identify as righteous jihadists, defending their faith and homelands from outside hostilities. In their eyes, the United States desecrates Islam by invading Muslim countries and supporting Israel in their Palestinian land grab.

A Jewish military chaplain I spoke with explained to me that, for a long time, Jews, Arabs, and Christians coexisted in the region. But then the Europeans came, and their colonization efforts created our current problems. The Europeans disrupted distinct tribal and religious sects, grouping them in makeshift borders, thus creating today's sectarian violence. The Middle East is dominated by Islam, which is experiencing two separate internal divisions, one between the Shiites and the Sunnis, and the other between moderates and fundamentalists. Iran is predominantly Shiite, as is Iraq. We handed Iran a gift when we took out Saddam, giv-

---

1   "What we fight," October 24, 2001.

ing Iran an opportunity to control another Shiitte country. Meanwhile, Saudi Arabia doesn't trust Iran, and it definitely doesn't want an Iran-dominated Iraq next door.

Then there's the struggle between the Arabs and the Jews. The Arabs, who are predominantly Muslim, have resented the Jews since the creation of the State of Israel in 1948. That resentment feeds the jihadists. The holy sites in Jerusalem—Israel's contested capital—are just as important to Muslims as they are to Jews. The Arabs also feel that the Palestinians were forced from their home by the Europeans to make way for Jews, who lay claim to the land because, according to their tradition, they're the descendants of Isaac, who settled there 4,000 years ago. Meanwhile, the Arabs counter this argument by saying that they are the descendants of Isaac's father, Abraham, who lived there 6,000 years ago. Both Sunnis and Shias view the United States as an adversary because of our unwavering support of Israel, and for propping up what they see as puppet governments in places like Kuwait, Jordan, and Egypt. Another reason for their disdain was our taking their oil.

Our position in the Middle East is also heavily influenced by the fact that many American Christians believe God promised Israel to the Jews, and that therefore the Jews are the rightful owners of the Holy Land. Former Republican Congressman Mike Conaway from Texas, a member of the Select Intelligence and Armed Services Committees, went on record saying he supported Israel for this very reason. "I'm pretty straightforward," Conaway said on the May 31, 2012, episode of C-SPAN's *Washington Journal*. "I read the Old Testament. God will bless those who bless Israel, and curse those who curse Israel. So, I am going to back Israel."

***

The neocons devised the "War on Terror" to persuade Americans into thinking that invading Iraq was a just decision. But rather than stopping terrorism, this war has only fueled animosity toward the United States and the West. Bush thought nothing of invading Arab countries and killing thousands of innocent people, but then he expected them to fling their arms open to welcome us as heroes and liberators. That makes zero sense. What Bush did was further enrage the extremists. It was this frustration toward American arrogance that instigated the infamous shoe-throwing incident during Bush's last presidential visit to Iraq on December 14, 2008. The jihadists know they can't defeat us through military means, so they rely on terrorist tactics. If we continue this "War on Terror," we will be chasing ghosts forever.

CHAPTER 13

Pawns of the Deadly Betrayal

"Military men are dumb, stupid animals to be used as pawns for foreign policy."
—alleged statement made by Henry Kissinger, secretary of state during the Vietnam War, as reported by Bob Woodward and Carl Bernstein in their book *The Final Days*

On October 13, 2006, I observed a group of wounded warriors, veterans of the Iraq and Afghanistan wars, on a tour of the Pentagon. Among them was a melancholy young man in a wheelchair who looked as though he may have just turned eighteen. One of his legs was amputated and he wore a patch over one of his eyes. I went over to him, said hello, and asked him how he was doing. He responded with a gloomy "OK" and went about his way. Then I saw an Air Force sergeant painfully walking with a limp, his entire face badly burned. Tears welled up in my eyes. At that moment, it hit me that those valiant souls had no idea why they had made their sacrifice. I decided right then and there to start asking service members if they knew why they were asked to invade Iraq, considering that no WMD were found. One of these conversations, with decorated Iraq and Afghanistan war veteran Lieutenant Colonel Greg Harbin, has stayed with me throughout the years.

"Why do you think we were asked to pull up stakes in Afghanistan and head off to Iraq?" I asked Harbin.

"Chief," he responded, "I wear this patch over my eye because of the war, and left part of my brain over there due to a traumatic brain injury, and to this day, I still don't know why I was asked to go." He then added, "I never felt it was about WMD."

***

I see our service members for who they truly are: valuable human beings, not boots on the ground. They are someone's son or daughter. Husband or wife. Mom or dad. Brother or sister. More than 4,500 of them made the ultimate sacrifice, and 100,000 have been wounded for life. There were no weapons of mass destruction in Iraq. Saddam Hussein posed no threat to our national security. The Iraq War wasn't an honest mistake. It was a calculated lie—a deadly betrayal. Our service members were used as pawns by the government to fulfill an imperialist ideology. Their sacrifice had no basis in national defense. All Americans should be outraged, and we should never let this happen again. The troops didn't even know why they were going to war.

Over the years, I would periodically return to my hometown, Fayetteville, North Carolina, and visit Fort Bragg Army Post, located a few miles outside of town. The facility (which was renamed Fort Liberty in 2021[1]) is home of the XVIII Airborne Corps, 82nd Airborne Division, and the Army Special Operations Command. These were Army units that made significant contributions to the war effort. I would walk up to soldiers and introduce myself as an old E-9, command sergeant major type. I used language that was equivalent to my Air Force rank, which I knew they would recognize. I would then ask, "Why were the troops asked to go to Iraq?" To ensure I had a good sampling, I would relay that same question to airmen, marines, sailors, and soldiers in Washington, D.C., at the Pentagon, Air Force bases, and at Walter Reed Medical Center. Each time, I would get the same puzzled look

---

1   This was brought about by the William M. (Mac) Thornberry National Defense Authorization Act, which established a commission for renaming Department of Defense properties named after Confederate leaders.

and response: "I really don't know why," or "We were told it was about weapons of mass destruction, but we never found them," or "I believe it was about revenge for the president's father," or "I believe it was about oil."

"I believe." "I think." "I don't know." These were the words I would constantly hear from hundreds of military men and women. One group of soldiers admitted to me that they felt betrayed because no WMD were found. In 2006, three years into the war, an airman who was assigned to a medical unit in Iraq told me, "While under enemy fire and attempting to offload some wounded personnel from a helicopter, I kept asking 'where are those damn WMDs?'"

***

During the last ten years of my military career, I was a senior leader responsible for providing feedback to the Department of Defense's top brass in regards to the needs, readiness, and morale of the more than 100,000 men and women of our armed forces and their families. I was a tireless advocate for our troops and developed an outstanding reputation among them. Every opportunity I got, I went to my fellow senior leaders and told them what we owed the troops and their families: pay raises, housing, medical benefits, fair treatment, prestige. Our service members are exceptional people, and I knew that one day, I might have to put them in harm's way for our country. But I never imagined something like this.

The conflicts in Afghanistan and Iraq became my worst nightmare. As you know by now, I was confused—not to mention perturbed—by the Bush administration's decision to send our troops off to fight a fabricated war. And I was furious each time I heard the neocons talk about how we need to support our troops—the very same troops, mind you, that they betrayed by using them as pawns. The neocons' remarks were nothing but empty sound bites.

During a March 2008 interview on ABC News, Dick Cheney responded dismissively to a question about how the Iraq War burdened the men and women of the military. "Oh, well," Cheney said. "They volunteered." Worse still, he then went on to claim that it was President Bush who carried the greatest burden. I don't think Bush's life was ever on the line during the entire conflict.

***

We can't keep sending our troops to fight unwinnable wars. To me, this amounts to inflicting physical and mental abuse on our service members. Our guard units were abused because we didn't have a large enough active-duty force. Our military is an all-volunteer force. If we look at the makeup of our recruits, we will find that a disproportionate number of them come from disadvantaged backgrounds. Most people join the military to escape poverty and to earn educational benefits. Some enlist seeking adventure and self-discovery. But pure patriotism isn't a driving motivator. If the Iraq War was truly a war of necessity, then all socioeconomic classes should've been appropriately represented in the Armed Forces. But that's far from the case. In fact, if there were still a draft, we would probably have fewer wars because all classes would be impacted.

In March 2008, we had 12,235 soldiers subjected to stop-loss orders. This meant that service members whose enlistment terms were up weren't permitted to end their service obligations. Instead, they were told to remain on active duty, based on a backdoor draft. Simply put, our government was holding our troops hostage, forcing them to remain the pawns of a fraudulent war. Does this sound like supporting our troops?

A continuous deployment with extended durations, without a clear objective, without a withdrawal plan, without an ending, doesn't support our troops. How long could we have expected them to go on like that? Many soldiers were killed or left severely wounded. Others had reached their emotional limits and were mentally battered. I saw many of these folks daily at Walter Reed. How can sending troops on fifteen-month deployments, on back-to-back rotations to a war zone with temperatures over 100 degrees and lacking proper protective equipment, be considered supporting the troops?

Unbelievably, the justifications from the neocons and their allies continued. On June 11, 2008, Republican presidential nominee John McCain said, "It is not important when the troops come home . . . as long they are not dying." McCain believed that if American troops were able to remain stationed in Europe, Japan, and Korea for decades, they ought to do the same in Iraq. Sadly, I don't think McCain ever really understood how dangerous it was for our troops to stay so long in Iraq—or anywhere else in the Middle East, for that matter—because of the Arabs' hatred of Western colonialism and occupation, a hatred that has given extremists the ammunition to further target our service members.

***

In December 2004, Donald Rumsfeld traveled to Kuwait to visit a deployment center where hundreds of soldiers were stationed, awaiting assignment to Iraq. While there, an Army specialist took Rumsfeld to task. He was worried about his platoon's vehicles, which weren't properly armored, so he asked the secretary of defense what he was planning to do about it. The specialist's question was greeted with thunderous approval from the crowd. After all, many service members had lost their lives or were severely injured due to the dearth of protective vests and unsafe Humvees that lacked armor. Rumsfeld's response? "You go to war with the army you have, not the one you wish you might have." Now, I would agree with him if we were indeed fighting a war of necessity. But this was far from the case. Rumsfeld's response showed his complete disregard for our troops' concerns.

I was shocked when President Bush rejected a 3.5 percent pay raise for our enlisted members in 2008. He said three percent was sufficient. Though we were only talking about half a percentage point, that bump could've been a real morale booster. Of all people, Bush, who had ordered the troops to war and extended their deployments, should've led the charge for a bigger pay raise. Meanwhile, the neocons pulling the strings were pocketing millions off the war.

I also believe that we owe our military an opportunity for a better life when they return from war. To put it in perspective, when I enlisted in 1975, right at the tail end of the Vietnam War, I didn't have to pay a dime into my educational benefit fund, which covered tuition, books, and even some living expenses. I absolutely guarantee you that the soldiers fighting in Iraq and Afghanistan in the early aughts were more stressed than I ever was, and worked a lot harder than I ever did. From 1984 to 2008, military folks were under an educational benefit system called the Montgomery GI Bill. Service members had to contribute to their own college funds. The money they received after leaving the military wasn't enough to cover college expenses, let alone food. The Montgomery GI Bill was essentially a cost-cutting measure. On average, recipients received about $5,800–$9,600 a year when the average cost of a college education at the time was about $17,000 a year. Virginia Senator Jim Webb thought this was unfair to all the men and women who were putting their lives on the line. So, he sponsored a new measure, the Post-9/11 Veterans Educational Assistance Act of 2008. Webb's goal was to provide the deserving veterans of Afghanistan and Iraq access to more benefits that would better equip them when they left the military.

But the Bush administration didn't agree. Believe it or not, the neocons argued that providing a better benefit was too costly. Plus, they thought it would encourage troops to drop out of the military and enroll in school. In other words, if the troops could get out of stop-loss, they wouldn't agree to be used as pawns of an unprovoked war.

"The incentive to serve and leave may outweigh the incentive to have them stay," said Robert Clark, former Assistant Director of Accessions Policy at the Pentagon. If the troops supported the war, then why would they leave? And, more importantly, if they supported the war, why was the Bush administration so hesitant to offer them better benefits? Bush and his surrogates, including John McCain, refused to endorse Senator Webb's bill. What surprised me the most about McCain was that he admitted that he hadn't read the bill, but still refused to back it. How on earth did McCain, a Vietnam War veteran and POW to boot, not have the time to go over such an important measure? Thankfully, a deal was reached and the bill passed in 2009. Among other perks, the Post-9/11 Veterans Educational Assistance Act included a provision allowing military personnel to transfer some of their benefits to their immediate family members.

My idea of "supporting the troops" was not the President of the United States vetoing a bill that authorized a pay raise for the troops during time of war, just so that he could prevent seventeen former POWs and their families from collecting a judgment awarded to them by a federal court against Iraq, which had imprisoned and tortured them. It's hard to fathom, but Bush sided with the Iraqi government against our own military members because Iraq threatened to withdraw billions of dollars in oil money that it had invested in American banks if he were to sign the bill. Meanwhile, the United States had already spent nearly $30 billion to help rebuild Iraq, and Congress had approved an additional $16.5 billion. Basically, Bush was OK supporting Iraq financially, but denied our service members the damages they deserved for the torture they endured fighting for our country.

***

Many service members suffered because of burn pits in Afghanistan and Iraq, resulting in decades-long medical issues. While working at Walter Reed, I was approached by a number of veterans seeking help with undiagnosed illnesses and respiratory issues associated with their proximity to the burn pits and oil fires in Iraq. They were frustrated because no one believed them or understood what they were experiencing, and they didn't know how to prove that they were sick due to toxic exposures.

It took until 2022 to get a law passed that provided compensation. The PACT Act was a real victory, and it should be cheered by all. However, I find it frustrating that the normal gamesmanship had to play out before Congress passed the bill. Although some members of Congress had no problem sending troops to risk their lives, they balked at the thought of taking care of them after they returned. I'm outraged that we can secure the funds to fight wars, but not the money to care for those combat veterans who came back with severe health issues.

Because I fought hard to improve the living conditions of our troops, I was accused by some of my peers of loving the troops too much. Well, I'll say now what I said to them then: if loving the troops too much is wrong, then I do not want to be right. I will do everything I can to prevent our government from ever again using our service men and women as their pawns in an unjustified war.

CHAPTER 14

Is Our Foreign Policy Safe?

Our foreign policy revolves around our official relationship with other sovereign countries and non-state agents—including rebel forces, militias, warlords, and even terrorist organizations such as Al-Qaeda and the Islamic State. These relationships inform our national security strategy, which is developed to achieve objectives that contribute to our defense.

Historically, American foreign policy has centered on aggression, provocations, threats, and saber-rattling rather than diplomacy and empathy. I came across a surprising statistic that said the United States has been at peace for less than twenty years total since its inception. This doesn't jive with our self-portrayal as a peace-loving nation. Our current foreign policy is downright dangerous. In fact, it could very well annihilate the world. It's important to examine our foreign policy to see why this is the case and how we can improve it.

The Middle East

Since 1990, beginning with Desert Storm, we have been in a continuous military conflict in the Middle East. Though that campaign was to remove Iraqi forces from Kuwait, our primary interest in the Middle East is political and our goal is to ensure Israel's security. The Arab world is furious with our one-sided support of Israel and our lack of regard for the Palestinian people; this negatively affects our national security and foreign policy. Israel isn't totally blameless in the Middle East conflict. It's guilty of wrong-doing in its treatment of the Palestinians, something our government willfully overlooks. We provide Israel with more than $3.7 billion a year in support. Yes, Israel has a right to defend itself, but the United States should never have ordered our troops to fight a war in Iraq on Israel's behalf, nor should we do so in the future if hostilities break out in Iran or Syria.

We're also in the middle of a tug-of-war between the Shiites and the Sunnis. As previously stated, we are partly responsible for the instability in the Middle East. We took out Saddam by force, and through NATO, supported the overthrow of Libyan leader Muammar Gaddafi in 2011. Our actions led to destabilization, the birth of ISIS, and the continued spread of terrorism. We worsened the Syrian refugee crisis by funding and arming Syrian opposition forces because we wanted to get rid of President Bashar al-Assad. This has caused more death and more destruction. Assad isn't going to relinquish power easily, especially not after seeing what the United States did to Iraq and Libya. Iran won't give up its ballistic missile program, and our actions may force it to build nuclear weapons for protection against the United States and Israel. It would probably be prudent for Iran to do this. More nuclear weapons won't make the United States or the world safer, but our aggressive presence in the Middle East has led us to this probability. In good faith, Iran abided by the nuclear deal. However, we broke the agreement, sanctioned Iran, and threatened it with military action after it had agreed to a peaceful plan.

We need to change our overall strategy in fighting terrorism. Our current methods are neither sustainable nor realistic. The Bush administration made a major mistake by portraying the tactics used by international, mob-like organizations such as Al-Qaeda as military operations instead of as criminal acts, framing the struggle this way so it could launch a war in the Middle East. We don't have the unlimited resources to support a global "War on Terror," unless we're willing to reinstate the draft, invade and occupy countries forever, and raise taxes to fund these invasions. Terrorism is ideological; we cannot defeat it solely through military efforts. We are mistakenly using our armed forces to find and kill so-called terrorists in Afghanistan, Iraq, Syria, Pakistan, Yemen, and Africa. We currently have an illegal military presence in Syria under the disguise of fighting terrorism. Syria isn't a threat to our national security and we have no right to infringe on its sovereignty.

Though terrorists can strike fear and inflict damage, they aren't an existential threat. They cannot destroy the United States. The "War on Terror" hurts our readiness and definitely doesn't make us safer. Rather than spreading our resources thin by fighting terrorists around the world, let's concentrate on our homeland defense instead. This requires good intelligence, and the intelligence community and law enforcement agencies working together to share information. We should stay vigilant by protecting our borders and implementing more stringent mechanisms for our immigration and visa programs. Also, we must return to treating terrorism as what it is: a law enforcement crime, meaning that terrorist activity should be investigated by the FBI. And if any planned acts of terrorism against the United States have originated overseas, we should counter the threat through covert operations led by the CIA, with the assistance of the military's Special Operations and other Pentagon assets. Large land invasions do not work against terror. The way in which we eventually got Bin Laden and his deputy, Ayman al-Zawahiri, are perfect examples of this strategy working. As I mentioned earlier, if the Bush administration had listened to the CIA's reports on the dangers of Bin Laden, we might not be paying for the 9/11 catastrophe today.

Twenty years ago, the Bush administration exploited the American people's fear of terrorism. They did so by manipulating the public into supporting an unjustified war to further its militaristic agenda in the Middle East. It appears we have accepted that strategy, as we witnessed in October 2017, when our troops were killed in Niger in the name of fighting terrorism. Why hasn't our government gone to war against the guns used in the mass killings of our citizens by fellow Americans? Whether our citizens are killed by a mentally disturbed person, a gang, or any ideological cause, murder is murder. However, we continue to sensationalize terrorism to further our foreign policy. I worry more about a deranged American with access to high-powered guns than I am of Islamic terrorists. Our government seems eager to combat terrorists, but it's always "too soon" to even discuss targeting domestic mass murderers.

The Pacific

All my extended overseas assignments were in the Indo-Pacific region, which led me to become especially well-versed in our foreign policy and relations in that part of the world. I also have a personal connection to the region: I was born in Japan, where my parents were stationed, and my son was born in the Philippines, where I was stationed.

The biggest challenge in the Pacific is our growing tension with China. Unlike the United States, China has a non-interventionist foreign policy; it tries to stay out of the business of other countries. However, our recent actions have caused it to reconsider this strategy. China's military buildup has been a major concern to American policy-makers. Furthermore, China is a growing economic force, a true global superpower. So, we can assume that China's buildup is due to its unease with the American presence in the Pacific—and how that might affect its security and interests—which is understandable.

If Taiwan were to declare independence, that could trigger a confrontation with China. We have an unofficial pact with Taiwan to help defend it if attacked. But China doesn't view Taiwan as an independent nation. On the contrary, it sees it as a rogue state that broke off from the mainland after the Communist takeover. To keep the peace, we must balance coexistence between Taiwan and China, while still maintaining our one-China policy. This is a delicate task requiring diplomatic tact. Yet these past few years, the Biden administration and some members of Congress have been pushing the envelope, enraging China by calling for a more open, independent relationship with Taiwan. If we can pre-vent Taiwan from declaring itself a separate state, I don't think China will initiate a conflict. After all, China depends on Taiwanese materials for its lucrative export business, so it really can't afford warfare with Taiwan.

At the same time, however, due to American provocation with regard to Taiwan, our tensions with China are higher than they've ever been. The Chinese believe that the United States doesn't consider or respect their interest in Taiwan, which China perceives as a domestic issue. And China is frustrated with the United States's attempt to contain its influence. These frustrations came to a head in August 2022, when former Speaker of the House Nancy Pelosi visited Taiwan, infuriating China. China has tolerated previous visits to Taiwan by other US officials. Pelosi's act was seen as an especially grave affront, however, because of her high status within the US government, being second in line to the presidency. China responded to Pelosi's visit forcefully. It carried out large-scale naval and air operations around Taiwan and fired off missiles near Taiwan-ese shores. Most troublingly, China cut off military-to-military dialogue with the United States and increased its cooperation with Russia. These actions do not make us safer.

We need to collaborate with the Chinese. If we play our cards right, they can become a great ally, and work with us to help maintain peace on the Korean Peninsula. After all, China was instrumental in brokering negotiations to try to end North Korea's nuclear program. Ultimately, China has its own interests on the Korean Peninsula: it doesn't want to see a unified Korea, as this could bring American troops right to its border.

As part of its military buildup, China has expanded its presence in the South China Sea, causing more tension with Taiwan, as well as with its neighbors Malaysia, Brunei, and the Philippines. The South China Sea is full of marine life and rich in natural resources, to which the above-mentioned countries have laid some claim. But instead of allowing these governments to work out their own problems, the United States has stepped in where it doesn't belong, sending ships and planes to survey the region—a show of force that could easily provoke China. This aggressive tactic concerns me. In my opinion, such displays of unwarranted force have only caused Russia and China to grow closer.

I've spent hours traveling with Chinese defense officials during their orientation visits to the United States. These officials told me that China is eager to work with us to resolve world issues. China doesn't want war; it wants to be our ally. However, China is also tired of our disrespectful interference into its internal affairs. China is expanding its military presence as a result of our actions. Again, I don't think that makes us safer. Instead of proving our might, we need to reach out a hand.

***

Our other critical foreign policy issue in the Pacific is our relationship with North Korea. Our questionable history of enforcing regime changes on sovereign countries, simply because we don't like their governments, has instigated the acceleration of North Korea's nuclear program. After all, Bush included North Korea on his "axis of evil" list—along with Iraq, Iran, Libya, and Syria—at the January 2002 State of Union address. If you're North Korea and you see what the United States did to Iraq and Libya, would you let go of your nuclear operations? I seriously doubt it. No matter how the neocons or other warmongers feel, we have to deal with a nuclear-equipped North Korea, until it decides to reverse its program based on its guaranteed sovereignty and security. But after the United States backed out of the Iran nuclear deal, I don't think North Korea is willing to engage with us on that matter. In their eyes, Americans can't be trusted, which doesn't make us safer.

My last assignment in the Pacific was as the senior advisor to the Commander of the Pacific Air Forces. I spent a lot of time in South Korea, reviewing the training, readiness, and quality of life of our troops, who were prepared to face North Korea if war were to break out on the peninsula. I would visit the Demilitarized Zone often, the border separating North and South Korea. Seoul, the South Korean capital, lies only thirty-five miles from the border, with a population of more than nine million. Osan Air Base, where thousands of American troops and their families reside, is only forty-eight miles from North Korea. If war were to break out, we would be unable to evacuate American non-combatants in time. Additionally, North Korea would perceive any sign of a significant evacuation as the first stage of an imminent American attack, which could trigger a major preemptive strike by the North Koreans.

Military threats won't work with North Korea. The only way to resolve the issue of North Korea's nuclear program is through peaceful negotiations. Moreover, these negotiations must include China and Russia, considering these tensions are playing out in their backyard. Most critically, we have to keep our arrogance in check and treat all parties with respect, including North Korea. Only then will we come up with real solutions for lasting peace.

Going Forward

The United States should absolutely defend itself in response to any attack. But our military posture should be defensive, not preemptive. Yet beginning with the Iraq War, we've become increasingly hostile, threatening military action rather than resorting to diplomacy. In the case of North Korea and Iran, we can't continue to bully them into submission: neither country will give in to our demands. Rather, I believe in a foreign policy rooted in respectful engagement and aggressive diplomacy. The way I see it, we must deal with other nations respectfully, establishing relationships with perceived adversaries, which is what Obama did with Iran and Cuba. I even agreed with Donald Trump's attempt to forge rapport with Russia; why provoke unnecessary tensions that could lead to global disaster?

We need to stay out of other countries' business and stop trying to influence their way of life. What concern of ours is it if President Assad stays or goes? There are many Syrians who support their president. Are we to disregard Syria's desires and remove its rightful leader? That would only cause the Syrians to lash out at Americans. Many countries probably wanted regime change for America during the Trump administration, but we had to wait it out. The United States must stop trying to shape the world according to its whims, especially when we need to work on strengthening our own fragile democracy at home. We must face the truth that our actions have harmed a number of countries: Iraq, Libya, Syria, and Yemen, to name only a few.

The world is far too complex for us to think we can police it alone. And, more importantly, we can't afford to do so. Our foreign policy blunders are the result of unrealistic efforts to remain the world's only superpower. Whether we like it or not, the United States must share the stage with China. If we are to reimagine our foreign policy, then we could then easily diminish our current tensions. And although the United Nations is not perfect, we need to work within its parameters, too. We don't have the resources, either financially or personnel-wise, to continue fighting these endless wars and win the so-called "War on Terror."

We need a common-sense foreign policy that will keep our hawkish impulses in check. Before going to war, Congress should call in every member of the Joint Chiefs of Staff and the combatant commanders, without the secretary of defense or any member of the civilian administration, and ask them point blank: "Is this a war to which we must commit? Is there an actual threat, and are we ready?" Congress cannot be strong-armed into rubber-stamping a war without just cause; it must do its part in providing oversight.

***

I love the United States. I have dedicated my life to serving this nation, and I will always fight for it. But each country—like each family—has its own rules. Some parents allow more freedom to their kids than others. Every country is different, and we must respect its laws and customs, no matter how undemocratic. Yes, we can show that our way of life is effective by modeling democracy and encouraging others to emulate it, if they so choose. However, we should never impose our will on other nations.

Bush's strategy was to push for democracy through military action. He thought brute force would make the world safer. His strategy was an unmitigated disaster. The only way to make the world safer is through diplomacy, negotiation, and fostering mutual respect. Other than that, we must let sovereign nations deal with their own problems. Of course, we should speak out and provide moral support for those seeking greater freedoms. But they must take the first step. They must do it on their own. In the United States, we overcame slavery and gained civil rights when the people said they had enough. We must learn how to talk to our enemies, to compromise without sacrificing our values. Belligerence can only do so much. The British Empire and the Soviet Union learned that the hard way. Their hubris failed them, and we are headed down that same destructive path.

Twenty years ago, we invaded Iraq without just cause, and now the neocons want us to do the same in Syria and Iran. Meanwhile, China has boosted its military presence in the Pacific, Russia has engaged in its own imperialist folly in Ukraine, and North Korea has accelerated its nuclear program. These governments have witnessed our past actions and don't trust our current motives.

It's perfectly fine to have pride in our country. We are a great nation. But we can't keep provoking other countries and not expect them to retaliate sooner or later. The United States is the most powerful and most influential nation in the world. Everybody knows it. What are we still trying to prove? Preemptive wars and hegemonic aggression will be our demise if we don't rein in our arrogance. Members of Congress and former Bush administration officials need to stop their posturing in how they talk about Russia, Iran, Syria, and North Korea. Their "macho" attempts aren't doing us any favors. It's counterproductive. All this grandstanding does is motivate other countries to stand up to us.

EPILOGUE

Can It Happen Again?

"In my opinion, any future defense secretary who advises the president to again send a big American land army into Asia or into the Middle East or Africa should have his head examined."
— Former Secretary of Defense Robert Gates

When Donald Trump was elected president in 2016, talks of hostilities toward Iran and North Korea resumed, just as they did with Bush prior to the Iraq War. Throughout the 2016 presidential campaign, the candidates were competing to prove who would be the quickest to send troops off to fight politically motivated wars, or how fast they would tear up the Iran nuclear deal. Most of the Republican candidates were for invading Syria, reentering Iraq, keeping forces in Afghanistan, and bombing Iran. On the Democratic side, Hillary Clinton suggested establishing a no-fly zone over Syria, deploying ground troops, and—echoing most of the Republican candidates—ousting Assad. It was during Clinton's watch as secretary of state that the United States supported Gaddafi's removal in Libya. She also voted for the Iraq War.

With Syria, the hawks claim the Islamic State is threatening us, that we must invade in order to defend ourselves. By now we know full well their actual goal: taking out Assad, simply because he's Israel's nemesis and we don't like him.

It looks as though the United States, Syria, and Russia were able to push ISIS out of Syria. I predict that next we will claim that we must remove Assad on behalf of the opposition forces and the Syrian people. After the Islamic State was banished from Syria, Nikki Haley, at the time the U.S ambassador to the UN, told CNN, "We're not done. Assad's days are numbered." I think Russia, which has strengthened its ties to Syria, has a different idea about Assad's future.

***

In 2003, the George W. Bush administration deceived the American people into supporting a needless attack on Iraq. 4,500 US military members perished in the conflict, more than 100,000 were injured for life, and $1 trillion was wasted on an oops-no-WMD-but-hey-we-got-Saddam war. Our service members went in thinking they were defending our country. Tragically, they were wrong. This was the ultimate betrayal.

There should be no subject that we cannot discuss openly, especially when lives are at stake. No other issue has affected our foreign policy more than the Iraq War, and our world standing has suffered because we destabilized Iraq, Syria, and Libya. We need to have an open discussion to ensure that nothing like this ever happens again.

As a proud American and a former military leader, I had to write this book to share my insights, because the misguided decision to attack Iraq twenty years ago will affect us for the rest of our lives. I was compelled to speak out because some politicians continue promoting the big lie that the Iraq War was a just cause. Meanwhile, the neocons are eagerly waiting in the wings, champing at the bit for their chance to continue their warmongering in Syria and Iran.

Some pundits claim the damage has already been done, that we should move on and not look back on the Iraq War.

I disagree. If we're not careful, history could repeat itself. In Iran. In Syria. In North Korea. I cannot stand idly by as the neocons attempt to betray us yet again on the backs of our service members and their families. My goal is to make sure this never happens. I hope this book will help us pay better attention to whom our elected officials select as their foreign policy advisors. Those who espouse an overly aggressive, overly militaristic stance could lead us into more futile wars that will bankrupt our country, damage our national security, and even lead us to total collapse.

We deserve better.

Acknowledgments

I want to thank God for putting me in the position, giving me the strength and insight to write this book. My family, who put up with me for more than ten years while I tried to put my thoughts on paper. Major Gen. (Ret.) Ted Mercer, for his inspiration and motivation; Philip Chevallard, former Commander of the Air Force Band of the Rockies, the first person who urged me to write a book; and Chief Master Sgt. (Ret.) Delamar Jones, another of the originals who encouraged me to write about my life and military career. Pastor Joel Osteen, for his motivational sermons every Sunday morning (in particular, the sermon that said, "Follow God's advice. We've missed out on great books that should have been written but were not, because people were afraid to follow visions sent by God"). Mister Jeff Kamen, for pushing me to be more passionate about my writing with his candid advice; and Larry Wilkerson, for his confidence in me. And a special thank-you to my father, the late Sam D. Fritz, who at age eight-nine stayed on me to not give up, and Mister William Graham, Sr., who at age ninety-five encouraged me and told me I had to finish this book. They both provided me with wisdom. And a very big thank-you to my man Jonathan Ambar, for all his hard initial editing work, and to Colin Robinson and the entire team at OR Books for taking a chance on my story. Finally, my deep thanks to all the men and women of our Armed Forces, for all their hard work and sacrifice.

About the Author

Dennis Fritz, director of the Eisenhower Media Network, is a former Air Force Command Chief Master Sergeant who retired from military service as a highly decorated and respected leader. He worked directly with and advised some of the most senior general officers in the Department of Defense. During his last decade of active-duty service, he held two of the Department of Defense's and the Air Force's highest enlisted positions: Senior Advisor to the Commander of Pacific Air Forces and Command Chief Master Sgt. of Air Force Space Command, with additional duty as the senior enlisted advisor to the Commander of North American Air Defense Command (NORAD) and the US SPACE Command. Chief Fritz also had the honor and privilege to serve as the senior enlisted leader and advisor to the commander of Andrews Air Force Base, the home for Air Force One, the world's most recognizable plane.

Chief Fritz also served at the Pentagon as an executive officer to then-Major Gen. Buster Glosson, the director of legislative affairs, Office of the Secretary of the Air Force, and architect of the air campaign during Operations Desert Shield and Desert Storm from 1990 to 1991, the first military operations against Saddam Hussein, under President George H. W. Bush.

After his active-duty service, Chief Fritz returned to the Pentagon to work in Donald Rumsfeld's Under Secretary of Defense for Policy Office, first as an administrative officer to the deputy assistant secretary of defense for Combating Weapons of Mass

Destruction and Negotiations Policy; later as a member of the Declassification Review Team for Pre–Iraq War Policy Planning Documents; and, finally, as a member of the Policy Planning Office in the Office of the Secretary of Defense (OSD), where he gained insights into the formulation of the defense strategies in support of President George W. Bush's national security strategy and policy following 9/11.

After leaving OSD, he continued serving his country and the military community from November 2008 to May 2022 as part of the Pentagon's official Wounded Warrior Care Program. He is a recognized expert in wounded warrior non-medical case management and for more than five years was the face of the Air Force at Walter Reed National Military Medical Center for the care and support of wounded warriors and their families. He fought to ensure our wounded warriors got the support and care they truly deserved. As a contracted program manager for the Army's Wounded Warrior Program, he traveled throughout the United States providing leadership and mentorship to Wounded Warrior Advocates and care coordinators who provide support services to the most severely injured military members at military treatment facilities, warrior transition units, and the Department of Veterans Affairs medical centers.

Chief Fritz has been featured on Black Entertainment Television's *Blacks in the Military* series and was listed and honored in the book *Black American Military Leaders: A Biographical Dictionary*. Along with his military achievements, he holds an executive master's in public policy management from the University of Maryland.